Extraordinary Outcomes Series
Book Two

for a Magical Life

Victoria Benoit

Extraordinary Outcomes Publishing, LLC
Phoenix, Arizona

ExtraordinaryOutcomesPublishing.com

Three *Magical* Words for a Magical Life™

Copyright © 2020 by Victoria Benoit

www.ExtraordinaryOutcomesPublishing.com,
Phoenix, Arizona

All rights reserved. No part of this book may be reproduced in any form without the written consent of the author except for brief citations in reviews or quotations. Proper credit must be given.

The author of this book never, either directly or indirectly, dispenses medical advice or prescribes the use of any techniques as a form of treatment for physical, emotional, or medical problems. In the event you use any of the information in this book for yourself, the author and the publisher assume no responsibility for your actions. For treatment of physical, emotional, or medical problems, see your physician or other health-care provider.

The intent of the author is to offer information of a general nature to help you in your quest for living a magical life. Most of the stories portrayed in this book are specific to the author's life. Names have been changed in all stories to keep people's identities private, with the exception of my beloved Bernie.

Contributors:
Cover Design, Line Editing, and Formatting: Betsy McGrew
Managing Editor: Paula Hofmeister
Portrait Photograph: Glenn Mire

Printed in the United States of America
Library of Congress Control Number 2021903755
Paperback ISBN 978-0-9838567-2-6
eBook ISBN 978-0-9838567-3-3

Three Magical Words for a Magical Life™ is a trademark of Victoria Benoit

*Book One in the
Extraordinary Outcomes Series
was dedicated to
my parents for their love and encouragement.*

*Book Two in the series is dedicated to
you, the reader, for your courage to heal
your past and live a magical life,
and
my late beloved husband, Bernie Klein,
for his dedication, love, and support
during our ten magical years together.*

Contents

Preface ix
Introduction xi
Living a Magical Life is Possible xi
How I Came to Write this Book xi
Chapter Overviews xv
  1 What Are the Three Magical Words? 1
  2 What About Forgiveness and Making Amends? 3
      Forgiveness 3
      Making Amends 4
  3 The Healing Process 7
      Healing Process with People Who Have Harmed You 8
      Healing Process for People You Have Harmed 10
      Integration 13
      Suggestions for Success 13
  4 Healing Your Relationships with Your Parents 17
      Healing Process with Your Parents 18
      Embrace the Healing 20
      My Healing Journey with My Mother 21
      My Healing Journey with My Father 23
      My Healing Journey for Harm I Caused My Father 25
      Final Thoughts 26
  5 Healing Your Relationships with Your Intimate Partners ... 29
      Healing Process with Your Intimate Partner 30
      Embrace the Healing 33
      My Healing Journey with an Intimate Partner 33
      Final Thoughts 35

Contents

6 Healing Your Relationships with Your Immediate Family 37
    Healing Process with Your Immediate Family 38
    Embrace the Healing 41
    My Healing Journey with My Siblings 41
    Final Thoughts 45

7 Healing Your Relationships with Your Extended Family 47
    Healing Process with Your Extended Family 47
    Embrace the Healing 50
    My Healing Journey with an Extended Family Member 50
    Final Thoughts 53

8 Healing Your Relationships with People in Your Community 55
    Healing Process with Community Members 56
    Embrace the Healing 58
    My Healing Journey with Community Members 59
    Final Thoughts 66

9 Healing Your Relationships with People at Work 69
    Healing Process with People at Work 70
    Embrace the Healing 72
    My Healing Journey with a Co-Worker 73
    Final Thoughts 75

10 Supporting Your Child(ren) to Heal Their Relationships and
Design Their Future 77
    Helping Your Child(ren) Heal Their Relationships 78
    Embrace the Healing 82
    Support Your Child(ren) in Designing Their Future 82
    A Child's Healing Journey 83
    Final Thoughts 85

11 Living a Magical Life 87

    Designing Your Magical Life 88

    Designing My Magical Life 91

    Manifesting Your Magical Life 93

    Manifesting My Magical Life 94

    Final Thoughts 99

Conclusion 101

Resources 103

Acknowledgments 105

About the Author 107

Stay Connected 109

About Book One 111

Preface

Magical lives are just that; magical, extraordinary, remarkable, exceptional, outstanding, incredible, phenomenal, unbelievable, amazing, astonishing, astounding, marvelous, fantastic, magnificent, wonderful, sensational, miraculous, fabulous, stupendous, out of this world, terrific, awesome, and wondrous. How is this possible?

It's possible by being curious, open, honest, loving, and humble. For those who are here to be all you can be—to love and be loved in profound ways and to make a meaningful difference in the lives of others—this book can be your ticket to these possibilities and more!

Using the three magical words with the people in your life and encouraging them to do the same, can have a global impact starting with YOU! Letting go of your past hurts and the harm you have caused others is the key. When your past is in the past where it belongs, you'll have a clean slate in the present to create and live a magical life.

During the twenty-five plus years I have provided Resonance Repatterning® and other transformational healing methods for my clients, I have found there is no hope in avoidance. Going into the unknown parts of yourself from your past may not be easy, however, it is necessary if you want to live a magical life.

May you have a sense of satisfaction and fulfillment as you read this book and implement the three magical words in your life.

Thank you for the opportunity and honor to make a difference in your life and in the lives of those who are blessed to have you in their lives.

Blessings of love and joy,
Victoria Benoit

Introduction

Living a Magical Life is Possible!

This book is about you and your life. It's designed for you to use three magical words to free yourself from past hurts that you've received and given. This can support you in emerging as your authentic self—to live a fully magical life!

When your past is unresolved, it not only impacts your life today, it also impacts your future. Your old thoughts and patterns will continue to show up in your life until you heal them. How can you create a magical life if your past is interfering?

This book is not for everyone. You will take an inner journey into some unhealed territory, but the rewards will be worth it—I promise. Some chapters may take more courage, especially the ones where you take responsibility for the hurt you have caused other people. The key is to have compassion for yourself and others.

At any time you become overwhelmed, I recommend seeking support or professional assistance. It's important that you take your time so you can integrate the positive changes you're making.

The more you allow yourself to explore unhealed areas within yourself, the greater the outcome. As you complete each process, it's important to take the time to notice the freedom you have created to live a magical life.

How I Came to Write this Book

The idea of this book came from a situation in my personal life with my late beloved Bernie. This is how it happened:

> *People who know me, know that I have a standard in my life about being on time. When I tell someone that I'll be*

somewhere at a certain time, I make sure I do what it takes to be there. I consider traffic and any stops I need to make (e.g. getting gas, picking up some wine) to determine what time I need to leave, and then I leave on time. If I realize I'm going to be even five minutes late—out of respect—I call the other person to let them know my new ETA.

During the time Bernie and I were not yet living together, and I knew he was coming over, I did a lot to make sure I was ready at the time he said he'd arrive. Bernie, on the other hand, was continually late and he never called to let me know.

I was getting increasingly frustrated when he'd show up late. Each time he'd say, "I'm sorry I'm late, I got distracted." Then, he'd go on and on, protecting and defending his tardiness with all his reasons and excuses, which were all valid to him—but not valid to me. It even got to the point where he wouldn't commit to a specific time so, in HIS mind, he'd be off the hook.

One day, I sat down with him and explained all the things I did to prepare myself to be ready and available at the time he said he'd be over. I told him, "I return all my phone calls. I finish the work projects I can complete. I clean my condo. I take a shower and pretty myself up. I get dinner started at the right time, so it's ready when you walk in the door."

I also told him, "I feel disrespected and dishonored when you are late. It makes me feel like you don't value my time, and your 'I'M SORRYS' just don't cut it anymore." He let me know that he had no idea the impact his tardiness had on me. I then asked him, "What are you going to do differently so this doesn't happen again?" He committed to leaving 30 minutes earlier than usual to make sure he would be on time. I let him know I thought that would probably work—BUT something was still missing.

What I needed from Bernie was for him to do something special that demonstrated to me that he was serious about making amends. By making it up to me, I could forgive him and we could release the past and move forward with a fresh start.

Bernie was masterful at making special—EXTRA SPECIAL. He took me to a fabulous, local five-star steakhouse as a way to reestablish our connection. We had a wonderful, loving experience.

From that day forward, Bernie honored his promise to not only be on time, but to be considerate, responsible, and accountable for the impact his actions—or lack thereof—had on me and others.

His earnest transformation allowed me the grace to heal my heart and restore my compassion for his humanity.

Working through this challenge with Bernie, I knew I had to write this book so others could benefit from the insightful healing process and create a magical life for themselves. May the outpouring of my experience provide wisdom that touches your life in profound ways.

Chapter Overviews

In **Chapter 1**, you will discover what the three magical words are and their importance.

Chapter 2 introduces different points of view about forgiveness and making amends.

Chapter 3 explains the **Healing Process** used in the chapters that follow.

Chapters 4-9 explore how to heal past hurts, both those you received and those you caused, in all the relationships in your life. This includes your parents, your intimate partners, your children and siblings, your extended family, your friends, teachers, coaches, clergy, etc., and your work associates.

For those who have children, **Chapter 10** will rock your world. This chapter illustrates how to support your children to heal with anyone who has caused them harm. In addition, ways to assist your children in articulating what they want in life and how they might go about getting it, are presented. Completing this chapter with your children can be a powerful support to them in having their dreams become reality.

Chapter 11 encourages you to create the magical life you intend to live, by using several approaches that will support you in designing and manifesting your intentions for your future.

This book is designed to encourage you to heal all the relationships in your life, beginning with those that are usually most impactful through those which, in many cases, have less significance. Although you can do this work in any order you choose, I recommend starting with your parents and continuing with each chapter at your own pace.

Balance is the key! As you are healing and making changes in your life, it's easy to become overwhelmed and frustrated. Be gentle with yourself, love yourself, and pace yourself. Take your time. This isn't a race. It's a journey into your inner world, where the limitations that stop you from living a magical life are patiently waiting to be transformed.

I'm often reminded that everyone is on their own path. People are in our lives for specific purposes; sometimes they are present only for a few weeks, several months, or many years; and some people stay forever.

A Reason, A Season, and A Lifetime

"People come into your life for a reason, a season, or a lifetime.
When you figure out which one it is, you will know what to do.
When someone is in your life for a REASON,
it is usually to meet a need you have expressed outwardly or inwardly.
They have come to assist you through a difficulty, to provide you with guidance and support, to aid you physically, emotionally or spiritually.
They may seem like a godsend, and they are.
They are there for the reason you need them to be.
Then, without any wrongdoing on your part or at an inconvenient time, this person will say or do something to bring the relationship to an end.
Sometimes they die. Sometimes they walk away. Sometimes they act up or out and force you to take a stand. What we must realize is that our need has been met, our desire fulfilled; their work is done.
The prayer you sent up has been answered and now it is time to move on.
When someone is in your life for a SEASON,
it is because your turn has come to share, grow, or learn. They bring you an experience of peace or make you laugh. They may teach you something you have never done. They usually give you an unbelievable amount of joy.
Believe it. It is real. But only for a season. And like Spring turns to Summer and Summer to Fall, the season eventually ends.
LIFETIME relationships teach you lifetime lessons;
things you must build upon in order to have a solid emotional foundation.
Your job is to accept the lesson; love the person or people involved; and put what you have learned to use in all other relationships and areas of your life.
It is said that love is blind but friendship is clairvoyant.
Thank you for being a part of my life."

~ Brian A. (Drew) Chalker

What Are the Three Magical Words?

"I never knew how strong I was until I had to forgive someone who wasn't sorry and accept an apology I never received."

~ Author Unknown

Many books have been written about magical words. The three words I want to reveal, you may not have previously thought were magical. Nevertheless, they are magical indeed! I bet you are wondering what the three words are. I bet even more, that you've already gone to the back of the book to find out what they are. I did the very same thing when I read, **Three Magic Words,** by U. S. Anderson. I thought for sure they would be, *I love you*, just as you may have thought about this book. Actually, it's much easier to say, *"I love you,"* than to say the three magical words, *"I am sorry."* Yet, as you will discover, it's more than just saying those words that makes the difference.

There may be many negative images and thoughts that come up for you when you hear, *"I am sorry."* You may have jumped all the way back to a childhood incident, such as being spanked while being told, *"I'm sorry,"* and decided that love hurts. Later, as an adult, you may have attracted a husband, a wife, or a partner to you that hurts you because of this subconscious belief.

It's important to release all your negative experiences associated with the words, *I am sorry,* so they can become magical words. To have a magical life filled with full self-expression, creativity, and joy it's important to heal the hurt and pain from the past. It's difficult to create and live a magical life if your unresolved past is unconsciously intruding. Going into the hurtful experiences from your past may not be easy, nonetheless, it is necessary if you want to live a magical life filled with love, adventure, passion, and joy.

What About Forgiveness and Making Amends?

"When you hold resentment toward another, you are bound to that person or condition by an emotional link that is stronger than steel. Forgiveness is the only way to dissolve that link and get free."
~ Catherine Ponder

At this point you may be asking, *"What about forgiveness?" "What about making amends?"* Good questions! That's what this chapter is all about.

Forgiveness

In a presentation I attended, Dr. Rick Hindmarsh said, *"I have been a physician for four decades and have seen more lives destroyed by bitterness than cancer, addiction, heart disease, diabetes, and contagious diseases combined."*

The moment we take on the harm of an incident, bitterness sets in, which can destroy us physically, emotionally, mentally, and spiritually. The way to release this bitterness is through forgiveness.

There are many approaches to forgiveness. I've outlined three of them here, that I use regularly.

Counseling Psychologist, Doreen Virtue, PhD. states, *"Forgiving someone doesn't mean what they did is okay, it simply means that you are no longer willing to hold onto any negative feelings in response to what happened—you don't have to forgive the ACTION, just the person—so you can be at peace."*

Another approach to forgiveness is called, exoneration. Stephen Marmar, in a Prager University video, states that, *"Exoneration can occur when a person is truly sorry for hurting you and takes full responsibility (without excuses) for what they did, as well as assures you that they will not do it again—it wipes the slate entirely clean and restores the relationship."*

I learned Bert Hellinger's **Family Constellation Forgiveness Theory** when I was expanding my coaching methods. His theory explains that it's not up to US to forgive. Since we generally want to have peaceful relationships, we unconsciously take on the pain caused by others, along with any guilt for their behavior—in the hope they will harm us less. Therefore, it's up to the person who caused the harm to take responsibility for their behavior and ask the Divine to forgive THEM. Our job is to energetically allow them to take back the guilt and pain they caused, so we can heal. The use of this approach is especially effective for people who have been abused.

Forgiveness is not a feeling, it's a decision. Keep in mind, forgiveness is different than trust. Forgiveness is granted. Trust is earned. Each path to forgiveness can be of value depending on your circumstances. I use a combination of all three methods of forgiveness in the following chapters.

Making Amends

To bear your soul and admit that you have made a mistake, or said something you regret, takes a big person. To honor another as you would like to be honored, and treat another as you want to be treated, is a special gift you bring to yourself and the other person. To be open and vulnerable takes a lot of courage. Be courageous—making amends is worth it.

When someone reaches out to make amends, be generous, listen, and let them apologize. It will set you both free. Remember to separate the person from their behavior—it'll be easier to let go of the hurt. It's also an opportunity for you to take inventory of what you did that might have hurt them and apologize.

Consider, we're all doing the best we can with all the negative experiences we've been through and the limited opportunities and options available to us to facilitate healing our hearts. The more information and transformational tools we have at our disposal, the more responsibility we have to use them.

Even though you know that we are all doing the best we can, it doesn't mean you need to stay in a relationship with someone who is abusive, hurtful, or who won't participate in resolving challenges.

The Healing Process

"Turn your wounds into wisdom."
~ Oprah Winfrey

This book is not just about saying the words, *"I am sorry,"* it's about having these three words make a positive difference in your relationships and your life. By taking your precious time to engage in the **Healing Process** presented in this chapter, you can free yourself to have a magical life. Here's the recipe I discovered that really works.

The **Healing Process** with those who have harmed you is slightly different than the one applied with those you have harmed. I have outlined each of them below.

I recommend that you create a notebook, journal, computer document, or other structure that works for you, as a system dedicated to your healing. You will want to organize your system so you can easily capture 1) what happened; 2) the name of the person(s) involved; 3) their relationship to you; 4) the age you were at the time; and 5) what you were feeling when it was happening. You may want to have a separate page for each person or just include the name and relationship with each incident. I will refer to this system as your *Healing Notebook*. Designate several pages for each chapter to quickly jot down recollections that come to mind.

The **Healing Process** will require you to recall information about each incident you want to heal. The process will work even if the person is deceased or no longer in your life at all.

Every emotion is stored in every cell of our body. Now is the time to release any harmful emotions from your past so you can heal and move forward in your life. Louise Hay authored a wonderful book, **You Can Heal Your Life,** in which she identifies that stored negative emotions cause a wide variety of unpleasant symptoms and physical ailments in the body.

Sometimes, examining harmful recollections is difficult. You may feel the need to be supported on this journey. Don't hesitate to have someone you trust—a friend, clergy member, or professional counselor—available to make this process safe for you. It's important to know that you indeed survived these hurts. Although you cannot undo what happened, you can energetically release the harm that you've been harboring for years. This does not, however, excuse your behavior or the behavior of others.

The degree to which you participate in this healing work is the degree to which you will free yourself from the past. You will then have more room in the present to experience love, optimism, hope, and peace of mind to create a magical future filled with new possibilities, beyond what you ever imagined.

As you begin each healing session, it's important that you bring your energy and awareness into your precious heart. This makes authentic forgiveness and amends possible.

To get the most out of this journey, set aside enough time to allow yourself to go deep into your inner knowing—where all your answers are. Find a private place where you won't be interrupted. Get comfortable and close your eyes. Center yourself in the present moment by taking a few deep breaths—slowly in and out through your nose. This activates your parasympathetic nervous system, which will cause you to be calmer and more relaxed.

There is genuine value in doing this with everyone who has harmed you or who you have harmed. It will not only set you free, it will set them free as well. Wow, what an opportunity!

Healing Process with People Who Have Harmed You

The **Healing Process** with people who have harmed you has four elements: 1) recalling and recording incidents from your past; 2) releasing your associated feelings; 3) energetically giving the responsibility back to the other person; and 4) receiving the other person's sincere apology.

Recalling and Recording

In each relationship category, in Chapters 4-9, recall an incident where someone harmed you with as much detail as you can. Using your *Healing Notebook*, record what happened along with the person's name and their relationship to you. Remember to include the age you were and your feelings at the time. You might start by saying, *"I'm ready now to face and heal my past hurts,"* then, accept whatever arises.

Your mind doesn't know the difference between what's real and what's imaginary. Don't spend time wondering whether something really happened—just work with it.

Releasing Your Feelings

As you recall each experience, allow your emotions to surface, as they most likely will. The feelings may include anger, betrayal, sadness, grief, humiliation, confusion, shame, etc. Whatever the emotion is, REALLY feel it and let it out.

For example, when you feel angry—really feel it and express it—go for a run, beat on some pillows, sit in your car and scream, or whatever works for you. The only rule is to not harm yourself or others. When the anger dissipates, it's likely that another underlying feeling will arise. Express this feeling just as vigorously. Keep expressing each underlying feeling as it arises until you experience a sense of freedom and calmness. Releasing your feelings begins the process of healing.

Freeing Yourself from the Harm

Now is the time to energetically free yourself from the harm by giving back to the other person the responsibility you've been assuming for their behavior. Close your eyes and visualize the other person standing in front of you. Say the following statement aloud:

> *"I'm giving you back the responsibility I've been assuming for the harm you caused me. By giving you back your responsibility, I'm also giving you back your dignity. I know you have the strength to carry it. Please, give me your blessings as I direct my energy and attention—which are now free—to create my magical life."*

Visualize the other person gladly receive your communication and imagine them saying to you—with honor and respect:

> *"It's no longer necessary for you to assume my responsibility for the harm I caused you and I accept the guilt for my behavior. I give you my blessings as you move forward in your life."*

I recommend copying these statements into your *Healing Notebook* so they're easily accessible when you're healing each experience.

Receiving an Authentic Apology

To complete the process, recall the incident you want to heal and the other person providing:

FIRST: A genuine, authentic and complete apology. For example:

> *"I am sorry for all the harm I caused you, when I said/did _____."*

THEN: Action(s) that ensure it won't occur again. For example:

> *"I'll speak respectfully so I don't cause you anymore harm."*

FINALLY: A way to restore the relationship. For example:

> *"How can I make it up to you?"*

Picture what you need—and VISUALIZE them doing it.

You may want to write down the imaginary responses and refer to them as a way to discover patterns.

Healing Process for People You Have Harmed

Doing this is all about using the **Healing Process** to liberate yourself from the guilt of any harm you caused—or think you caused—to other people in your life. Often, the way we have been harmed, is the way we harm others.

This is not for the accidental times you hurt someone. This is for the times when you were angry, jealous, afraid, or hurt and didn't know how to respond other than to take it out on the other person. It is for those times when you acted out, lied, cheated, tattled, stole, took the credit, shifted the blame, sabotaged another, etc. The survival ego part of you reacted rather than responded. That was you in the past. Now is now, and NOW is the time to let go and free yourself from these experiences. Free your heart. Free your mind. Free your soul.

No need to judge yourself harshly if you think there are too many people you have hurt, just love yourself, and pace yourself. This isn't a race. It's better to get everything out and in the process of healing than to keep it bundled inside. Take a couple of deep breaths and relax. This may not be as comfortable as healing with those who harmed you, although, you'll have a lot more energy available to you just by doing this. You'll have to trust me on this one.

The **Healing Process** with people you have harmed, also has four elements: 1) recalling and recording the incidents; 2) releasing your associated feelings; 3) energetically taking back the responsibility and guilt; and 4) giving your authentic and sincere apology.

Recalling and Recording

For each relationship category, in Chapters 4-9, recall an incident where you harmed another. In your *Healing Notebook*, include your age and what happened in as much detail as possible (i.e. what you did or didn't do—what you said or didn't say), as well as the person's name along with their relationship to you.

You might start by saying, *"I'm ready now to face and heal the harm I have done to others,"* then, accept whatever arises. Remember, your mind doesn't know the difference between what's real and what's imaginary. Don't spend time wondering whether something really happened—just work with it.

Releasing Your Feelings

As you recall each experience, allow your emotions to surface. Whatever the emotion is, really feel it and let it out.

For example, when you feel remorse, regret, grief, sadness, shame, embarrassment, or anger—REALLY feel it and express it—cry, journal, punch your pillow, whatever works for you. The only rule is to not harm yourself or others. Keep going until you experience a sense of freedom and calmness. Releasing your feelings begins the process of healing.

Taking Back the Responsibility and Guilt

It's time now to energetically free the other person from the harm you caused by taking back the responsibility and guilt for what happened. Close your eyes and visualize the other person standing in front of you. Say the following statement aloud:

> *"I take back the responsibility and accept the guilt for the harm I caused you. It is no longer necessary for you to assume this responsibility. I give you my blessings as you move forward in your life."*

Visualize the other person gladly receive your communication and imagine them saying to you—with honor and respect:

> *"I appreciate the generosity and courage it took for you to admit that your unkind behavior offended me deeply."*

I recommend copying these statements into your *Healing Notebook* so they're easily accessible when you're healing each experience.

Offering an Authentic Apology

To complete the process, recall the incident you want to heal along with the person you harmed and provide the following:

> FIRST: A genuine, authentic and complete apology with no excuses or equivocation. For example:
>
> *"I am sorry for disrespecting you. You didn't deserve that."*

THEN: Action(s) that ensure it won't occur again. For example:

"I promise to be kind, considerate, and honest in the future."

FINALLY: A way to restore the relationship. For example:

"How can I make it up to you?"

Picture them telling you what they need—then you COMPLYING. Imagine the other person accepting your blessings.

Integration

After healing each experience, it's a good idea to be gentle with yourself and take some time to embrace that healing. Breathe deeply through your nose, which will help you to relax. Breathe in love and breathe out any tension that you may be holding in your body.

I suggest taking a break before you go right into the next person. You might want to write in your *Healing Notebook* about your experience of using the **Healing Process** and how you feel at this point.

After you've integrated the healing between you and others, you may see positive, loving actions to take with people in your life.

Suggestions for Success

Remember to pace yourself. Rome wasn't built in a day. Whether you process one incident per day, per week, or per month really doesn't matter. What matters the most is completing this process in the time that works for YOU. Be sure to give yourself some integration time between each person and acknowledge yourself for the courage it took to heal your relationship.

Acknowledging Yourself

At the end of each healing session, whether you have healed with one person or a dozen, I highly recommend doing something special to acknowledge yourself for the courage it took to heal with people in your life. Doing this will feed your soul and provide support as you continue this work. You are one of a small group of people who are doing what it takes to create a magical life.

Contacting People

When there is someone in your life who means a lot to you, and who you know has the capacity to listen and take responsibility, you may want to share what you are up to and the work you've been doing. Let them know that you're in the process of creating a magical life and it requires being responsible and accountable for forgiving harm you have caused others, and forgiving those who have caused harm to you. In so doing, you've discovered some hurt feelings in your relationship with them. Ask whether they would be open and willing to participate in a forgiveness process. If they agree, it provides an opportunity for them to communicate, open their heart, and grow in their capacity to love and be loved. It's a win-win for both of you.

If they say yes, set up a time to get together, by phone or in person (do not do this through email or text). If they say no, don't take it personally or get discouraged, allow them to be how they are at the moment—they may change their mind and contact you later.

Patterns

As you are healing incidents in your life, you may see patterns of behavior that happened with multiple people. If this occurs for you, I recommend doing a **Healing Process** with everyone who comes to mind that fits the pattern. You might even heal them all at once.

For example: I used this process to heal my relationships with five friends, all of whom had harmed me in a similar way, I realized the pattern began with never forgiving my father for packing up and leaving the family without an explanation. I healed that as soon as I saw it. As a result, since I did that work, the pattern has not reappeared.

Priority

I recommend that you put a priority on resolving your past experiences. Schedule time regularly until you have healed and feel peaceful. As you make the effort to heal each incident, notice how much freer and lighter you feel. You may experience life flowing naturally with more playfulness, fun, and ease. Observe how things open up for you in many areas of your life—it could be in your finances, your relationships, your health, your business, your creativity, etc. Over time, you may come to realize that all the areas of your life are becoming richer, fuller, and more meaningful. This will encourage you to keep up the momentum.

I predict, that the more you accomplish and the more you experience the personal power and freedom available to you, the more eager you will be to keep going. I trust that you will see the significance of doing the **Healing Process** with each person, as you design your magical life.

Healing Your Relationships with Your Parents

"Forgiving my parents didn't excuse their behavior, but it allowed me to move past the hurt."
~ *Tracey Casciano*

To have a magical life—filled with magical experiences, magical people, magical creativity, a magical career, magical moments with your children, friends, colleagues, neighbors, spouses, lovers, etc.—you must heal your relationships with your parents first.

In this chapter, you will be applying the **Healing Process** to your maternal and paternal relationships including: your biological parents, step-parents, adoptive parents, foster parents, and anyone else who you would describe as a parent. When I refer to your mother and your father, it includes all these categories.

In the event that there was abuse from any parental figure, I understand you may be reluctant to even consider using the energy it's going to take to come to terms with and heal the wounds. Doing this healing work does not mean you necessarily need to have anything to do with them ever again. You may, however, be surprised what positive outcomes can happen just from doing your own healing—not only in your relationships with anyone you consider a parental figure—but in all areas of your life.

You can never separate yourself from the sperm of your father and the egg of your mother—whether they are known to you or not—and no matter how far you try to distance yourself from them, you will always be a product of them. I recommend starting this process with your biological parents.

It's time to heal your relationship with your parents. As you heal each experience with your parents, notice how you feel. You may feel lighter in spirit and more free to be yourself. You may also notice that many areas of your life begin to open up and become easier. Remember to schedule time regularly until you have healed all the hurtful experiences with your parents and feel peace within.

Healing Process with Your Parents

Get out your *Healing Notebook*. Create a separate page for each parental figure in your life. Choose the relationship you want to heal before you begin your session. Set aside the time you need. Find a quiet place where you won't be disturbed and get comfortable. Close your eyes and center yourself in the present moment by taking a few deep breaths through your nose.

Healing Harm Your Parents Caused You

   Recall and Record

RECALL the first time you were punished, ridiculed, humiliated, demeaned, etc., by the parental figure who harmed you. Whether they said, *"I am sorry"* or not, the harm was done.

RECORD what happened, their name and relationship to you, your age, and how the experience made you feel.

   Release Your Feelings

Allow the emotions to surface and as each feeling comes up, do the work to release it.

   Free Yourself from the Harm

It's time now to energetically free yourself from the harm associated with the experience. Close your eyes and visualize the parental figure standing in front of you. Say the following statement aloud:

"I'm giving you back the responsibility I've been assuming for the harm you caused me. By giving you back your responsibility, I'm also giving you back your dignity. I know you have the strength to carry it. Please, give me your blessings as I direct my energy and attention—which are now free—to create my magical life."

Visualize the parent gladly receive your communication and imagine them saying to you—with honor and respect:

"It's no longer necessary for you to assume my responsibility for the harm I caused you and I accept the guilt for my behavior. I give you my blessings as you move forward in your life."

Receive an Authentic Apology

FIRST: Imagine your parent genuinely saying, *"I am sorry for _____ (what I said or didn't say; did or didn't do)."*

THEN: Imagine them saying what positive actions they will take to ensure the harmful behavior won't occur again.

FINALLY: Imagine your parent asking, *"How can I make it up to you and restore our relationship?"* Picture what you need and visualize them doing it. Allow yourself to accept your parent's blessings.

Healing Harm You Caused Your Parents

Recall and Record

RECALL the first time you caused harm to a parental figure. Whether you said, *"I am sorry"* or not, the harm was done.

RECORD what happened, their name and relationship to you, your age, and what feelings you inflicted on them.

Release Your Feelings
Allow the emotions to surface and as each feeling comes up, do the work to release it.

Take Back the Responsibility and Guilt
It's time now to energetically free yourself from the harm associated with the experience. Close your eyes and visualize the parental figure standing in front of you. Say the following statement aloud:
> "I take back the responsibility and accept the guilt for the harm I caused you. It is no longer necessary for you to assume this responsibility. I give you my blessings as you move forward in your life."

Visualize the parent gladly receive your communication and imagine them saying to you—with honor and respect:
> "I appreciate the generosity and courage it took for you to admit that your unkind behavior offended me deeply."

Offer an Authentic Apology
FIRST: Sincerely say, *"I am sorry for _____ (what I said or didn't say; did or didn't do)."*
THEN: Imagine telling the parental figure what positive actions you will take to ensure the harmful behavior won't occur again.
FINALLY: Imagine asking your parent, *"How can I make it up to you and restore our relationship?"* Picture them telling you what they need—then you COMPLYING. Imagine your parent accepting your blessings.

Embrace the Healing—You to Your Parents, Your Parents to You

When you consider there are many, many reasons (e.g. emotional overwhelm, lack of support, inherited disciplinary customs, mental disorders, impatience, etc.)—which are not necessarily intentional—that explain a person's hurtful reactions and behaviors, you can begin to have compassion and forgiveness for yourself and others.

Integration is the key to healing. To assimilate all of the energetic renewal available, always allocate an adequate amount of time after healing the harm from each experience. Sit quietly, breathe deeply through your nose—which will help you to relax—breathe in love and breathe out any tension that you may be holding in your body.

Notice and feel the love you now have for your parents. Allow it into all the cells of your body. Let it permeate your whole being.

Feel free to write in your *Healing Notebook* about your experience of using the **Healing Process**—how you feel now, plus any actions you feel inspired to take.

My Healing Journey with My Mother

Growing up, I felt my mother had my destiny in her hands. So, I believed it was best to do and say what she told me to do and say—even though deep inside I knew it was wrong. One of the most hurtful things she did, when my parents separated, was to tell me horrible things about my father that I believed. I thought I had to reject my father to live peacefully with her. So, I spent very little time with him and when we were together, I was distant and looking for evidence that my mother was right. This left me feeling confused, anxious, and guilty because I loved my father. I got stuck with these emotions at age 12.

My relationship with my mother was turbulent, even through the 16 years I lived 150 miles away. After my second divorce, I moved across the country to stay with my mother until I could get settled. After I got a great job and a place to live, I moved out of my mother's place. It was then that I realized counseling was necessary for me to focus on healing our relationship.

I had been working diligently with my counselor to heal the many harmful incidents in my childhood relative to my mother. One day my mother came over to my apartment—

unannounced—to let me know she had lost her job and the only way she could survive was to move in with me. She told me all the things she had done for me throughout her life, and therefore I owed it to her to take her in. Regardless of how much work I had done to heal myself, I still just acquiesced and said, "Yes."

About an hour later at my counseling session, it was brought home to me that I had reverted emotionally to the little girl who always obeyed her mother—no matter what. I became determined not to do that.

When I got home, my mother was happily awaiting both my return and the prospect of living together. I mustered up the courage to tell her that coming to live with me would not work. I offered to pay her rent and help in any other way I could. Even in the midst of my fear about her reaction, I felt powerful and proud of standing up for myself. How I related to my mother after this, was never again driven by that little 12-year-old girl.

She told me I was an ungrateful brat, disowned me, and left. She called for several days afterword and was verbally abusive. Each time, I simply told her that if she could talk to me with respect, I would be glad to have the conversation, and that I was hanging up now. She eventually stopped calling, and we didn't speak to each other for about five years.

During this 5-year timeout, I continued to work with my counselor to heal all the incidents with my mother that were still impacting my life. Eventually, I reached a place where all the wounds of the little girl inside me were healed, and I felt free and at peace with my mother.

I worked to release the stored emotions and give the responsibility and guilt back to her. I visualized my mother communicating sincere apologies to me, starting with "I am sorry for all the things I did that hurt you. You didn't deserve that." I imagined her promising to get the help she needed to heal her past. With each incident, I energetically told her what I needed to hear from her and what she needed to do for me to restore the relationship, and I saw her doing what I asked.

At 40, I could look back— from an adult perspective—and put myself in my mom's shoes. I was able to feel compassion for what she was going through at the time and could understand some of the choices she made. There were many behaviors I did not agree with, which I generously released.

When I completed counseling and was feeling strong, I wrote down all the ways I had turned out great. I included all the positive skills, abilities, and strengths I developed and integrated into my life as a result of the responsibilities that my mother entrusted to me as a child. I filled a whole page!

Afterward, I reached out to my mother to ask if we could get together and talk. She said it would be a while before she was ready to see me, but she was willing to talk over the phone.

During the next year, we talked and worked through the issues we still had. I came to understand and have compassion for her. We each took responsibility for the harm we caused one another and when we were both ready, we met. The reunion was heartfelt and loving. We have been able to maintain a caring, respectful relationship most of the time.

I was her advocate as she transitioned into assisted living. She is now super appreciative of the time I spend with her which feels good to hear and feeds my soul.

My Healing Journey with My Father

After I completed the Healing Process with others in my community, I discovered a pattern where people abruptly ended their relationship with me without an explanation. It was then

I realized the pattern originated when my father left our family when I was 12. Why in the world would he leave me? I loved my father—he didn't want to leave me but he left nonetheless.

Growing up, it was apparent that my mom wore the pants in the family. Whenever I wanted something, I'd ask my dad and even though he'd say, "Yes," he'd always conclude with, "But it's up to your mother." She inevitably said, "No!"

At church, I'd hear that the man is the head of the household, but not at my house. I was very confused and didn't understand why my dad wouldn't take on the man's role in our family.

One Saturday morning when I was 12, my mom called a family meeting and announced that my dad was moving out. She offered no explanation as to why—and neither did he. He did, however, say he didn't really want to leave, but he felt it was best. I felt betrayed. I was stunned, scared, devastated, sad, angry—every emotion imaginable.

I realized that if he left, I'd end up being the one responsible for everything between the time I got home from school and when mom got home from work. She expected me to do the housework, make dinner, and babysit my younger sisters and brother. Without my father, I'd be on my own with no one to support me. I would have to end all my after-school activities. The fun times were over—forever!

I just wanted to pinch my dad's ear and say, "Wake up! Stand up for yourself. How can you let her walk all over you? Why won't you save our family? What about ME?" I felt it was time for him to be the man of the house—he failed me.

After my dad moved out, I withdrew any respect I had left for him. I would go to the scheduled visitations, where he usually catered to what my 3-year-old brother needed. What I needed—again—didn't seem to matter. I shut my heart to him.

Over the years, my mom was always harping about how weak, spineless, and inconsiderate he was, which I took on as true. When I was about 15, I started making excuses not to see him—I didn't get the point of spending time with him. We rarely got together after that, except for my birthday and holidays. It seemed to work just fine for me.

My parents eventually got divorced and each of them remarried. Over the next 45 years, as I became an adult, my dad and I were able to have some wonderful talks about life and became closer, until his death several years ago. Yet, I knew there was still something missing.

After recalling the details of what happened when he left home, I knew I was now ready to be free of my resentment and bitterness. Next, I visualized my dad in front of me taking back his responsibility and guilt for what happened. I imagined him saying what I longed to hear, "I am sorry I didn't stand up for you and our family. I allowed your mother to rule the roost because it was easier for me. I realize I could have worked harder to provide the support you needed. I know that my leaving without telling you why must have had a negative impact on you. Over the years, I've learned to be more assertive and now feel strong within myself. How can I make it up to you, Vicki?" I saw him giving me the support I needed by helping me organize my finances and giving me tips about where I should invest my money.

Doing this process helped me open my heart completely to my late father, and I now have a greater tenderness for him.

My Healing Journey for Harm I Caused My Father

Wanting to reconcile my relationship with my father began when I was 18. Even though I was still living with my mother, I felt an urge to talk to my dad and apologize for rejecting him when I was 12.

We met and took this wonderful two-hour walk on the bank of the Root River. I shared with him that the only way I knew how to survive living with mom, was to cut him out of most areas of my life. He shared his side of the story, which was completely different than my mother's story about him. I listened, listened even more, and came to some realizations about who my dad really was. We held hands, talked, and wept. I shared the impact some of his behaviors had on my life and the conclusions I came to because of them. He understood.

As we were talking, I took responsibility for the harm I had caused him, by withholding my love, affection and attention. At one point, we stopped in our tracks, looked each other in the eye and I told him how sorry I was for being so distant. He let me know that he understood what was happening and was waiting for this day to come—which came much sooner than he expected. I promised him, that I would do my best to include him in my life.

We parted that day with so much love in our hearts, and our relationship grew stronger every day.

Final Thoughts

It's never too late to heal your relationship with your mother and your father. For those whose parents are still living, it could be interesting to see what naturally happens in your relationship. Now that you've begun the process of healing your relationship with your parental figures—and the past is in the past where it belongs—don't be surprised if they reach out to you. Should there be anything left for you to say when they contact you, go ahead and communicate from your heart. No matter how the conversation ends up, it'll be more complete than before you began the **Healing Process.**

We are driven so often in life by what we experienced, felt, and learned as children. **This** chapter, in **this** book, using **this** process is the most profound and impactful way to heal your parental relationships and move powerfully forward into your magical life.

Remember to do something special for yourself as acknowledgment for the courage it took to heal the past with your parents and reclaim your birthright of a magical future.

Healing Your Relationships with Your Intimate Partners

"At the heart of mankind's existence is the desire to be intimate and to be loved by another."
~ Gary Chapman

Now that you have healed most of the hurtful experiences with your parents, you are ready to move on to the intimate partners in your life.

In this chapter, you will be applying the **Healing Process** to your intimate partners including: your first love, boyfriends, girlfriends, live-in partners, husbands, wives, significant others, and anyone else who you would describe as an intimate partner. When I refer to your partner, it includes all these categories.

Sometimes I think it's amazing that intimate relationships happen at all. They take courage and resilience. They are the riskiest of all relationships in our lives. They demand priority and they involve your whole heart.

We all grew up witnessing many aspects of our parents' relationship, some of which were less than optimal. Your parents may have shown each other love, affection, kindness, generosity, and forgiveness, or you may have witnessed physical, emotional, mental, spiritual, and even financial abuse.

As children, we develop conclusions about what constitutes intimate relationships and how they work. Often, we mirror the characteristics of our parents' relationship or we choose the exact opposite type of behavior when interacting with a partner.

In the day-to-day of intimate relationships, things happen that leave us feeling hurt, bitter, resentful, angry, betrayed, or even vengeful. When we keep these feelings inside and don't heal the wounds, the relationship is doomed to failure.

According to Bert Hellinger, one of the most painful experiences in a relationship is when you realize that the other person is giving back less than you are giving, and you are more invested in the relationship than they are.

When relationships end—especially when betrayal is involved—we shut our hearts and there's no room to cultivate a healthy loving relationship. Any new person has no chance with us because we are projecting the previous relationship onto them. It's of paramount importance that we heal the broken relationships from our past in order to move forward.

It's time to heal your intimate relationships. As you heal each experience with your partner, notice how you feel. You may feel lighter in spirit and more free to be yourself. You may also notice that many areas of your life begin to open up and become easier. Remember to schedule time regularly until you have healed all the hurtful experiences with your partner(s) and feel peace within.

Healing Process with Your Intimate Partner

Get out your *Healing Notebook*. Create a separate page for each intimate relationship in your life. Choose the relationship you want to heal before you begin your session. Set aside the time you need. Find a quiet place where you won't be disturbed and get comfortable. Close your eyes and center yourself in the present moment by taking a few deep breaths through your nose.

Healing Harm Your Intimate Partner Caused You

 Recall and Record

  RECALL the first time you were dismissed, shamed, assaulted, betrayed, etc., by the partner who harmed you. Whether they said, *"I am sorry"* or not, the harm was done.

RECORD what happened, their name and romantic relationship to you, your age, and how the experience made you feel.

Release Your Feelings

Allow the emotions to surface and as each feeling comes up, do the work to release it.

Free Yourself from the Harm

It's time now to energetically free yourself from the harm associated with the experience. Close your eyes and visualize the intimate partner standing in front of you. Say the following statement aloud:

"I'm giving you back the responsibility I've been assuming for the harm you caused me. By giving you back your responsibility, I'm also giving you back your dignity. I know you have the strength to carry it. Please, give me your blessings as I direct my energy and attention—which are now free—to create my magical life."

Visualize the partner gladly receive your communication and imagine them saying to you—with honor and respect:

"It's no longer necessary for you to assume my responsibility for the harm I caused you and I accept the guilt for my behavior. I give you my blessings as you move forward in your life."

Receive an Authentic Apology

FIRST: Imagine your partner genuinely saying, *"I am sorry for _____ (what I said or didn't say; did or didn't do)."*

THEN: Imagine them saying what positive actions they will take to ensure the harmful behavior won't occur again.

FINALLY: Imagine your partner asking, *"How can I make it up to you and restore our relationship?"* Picture what you need and visualize them doing it. Allow yourself to accept your partner's blessings.

Healing Harm You Caused Your Intimate Partner

Recall and Record
RECALL the first time you caused harm to an intimate partner. Whether you said, *"I am sorry"* or not, the harm was done.
RECORD what happened, their name and romantic relationship to you, your age, and what feelings you inflicted on them.

Release Your Feelings
Allow the emotions to surface and as each feeling comes up, do the work to release it.

Take Back the Responsibility and Guilt
It's time now to energetically free yourself from the harm associated with the experience. Close your eyes and visualize the intimate partner standing in front of you. Say the following statement aloud:

> *"I take back the responsibility and accept the guilt for the harm I caused you. It is no longer necessary for you to assume this responsibility. I give you my blessings as you move forward in your life."*

Visualize the partner gladly receive your communication and imagine them saying to you—with honor and respect:

> *"I appreciate the generosity and courage it took for you to admit that your unkind behavior offended me deeply."*

Offer an Authentic Apology
FIRST: Sincerely say, *"I am sorry for _____ (what I said or didn't say; did or didn't do)."*

THEN: Imagine telling the intimate partner what positive actions you will take to ensure the harmful behavior won't occur again.

FINALLY: Imagine asking your partner, *"How can I make it up to you and restore our relationship?"* Picture them telling you what they need—then you COMPLYING. Imagine your partner accepting your blessings.

Embrace the Healing—You to Your Intimate Partner, Your Intimate Partner to You

When you consider there are many, many reasons (e.g. substance abuse, being inconsiderate and disrespectful, low self-esteem, lack of impulse control, trust issues, jealousy, etc.)—which are not necessarily intentional—that explain a person's hurtful reactions and behaviors, you can begin to have compassion and forgiveness for yourself and others.

Integration is the key to healing. To assimilate all of the energetic renewal available, always allocate an adequate amount of time after healing the harm from each experience. Sit quietly, breathe deeply through your nose—which will help you to relax—breathe in love and breathe out any tension that you may be holding in your body.

Notice and feel the love you now have for your partner. Allow it into all the cells of your body. Let it permeate your whole being.

Feel free to write in your *Healing Notebook* about your experience of using the **Healing Process**—how you feel now, plus any actions you feel inspired to take.

My Healing Journey with an Intimate Partner

When I met Larry at work and our eyes met, it was love at first sight. We were both Juniors and attended the same high school. I remember it being a whirlwind romance leading up to him asking me to our Junior/Senior Prom. I was beyond delighted, all dressed up in a flowing formal gown with a delicate corsage of pink roses that matched my dress, being escorted by a handsome, athletic young man in a black tuxedo.

Over the summer, we remained devoted and committed. We went everywhere together, swimming in a nearby lake, riding bikes along the river, and hiking secluded woodland trails. Our relationship was the envy of all my girlfriends. Everything we did seemed beyond affectionate and very romantic, so much so, that he became my first lover.

Before we new it, summer was over and we were back at school, the leaves were falling, and winter was blowing in from the north. Larry was such a demonstrative guy. He carried my books, helped me put on with my fur-lined coat. He treated me like a queen for all to see.

That year the holidays flew by. Thanksgiving with my family was amazing, followed by the most awesome Christmas of my life. Before we knew it, Spring was here and our lunch hours were being spent at a friend's house across the street from the school so we could be together—alone.

One day another girl showed up at the house. When she saw Larry and I coming out of a bedroom, she exploded, "What are you doing with her? I thought you loved me." I was shocked and humiliated. I had no idea Larry was seeing anyone else while we were dating.

The cat was out of the bag. He was playing both of us! I felt so hurt and betrayed! At the time, I was so head over heals in love with him that—rather than breaking up with him—I demanded that he choose, "It's me or her." I assumed he would choose me—I was wrong, he chose her. Ouch!

Over the next few days, it was difficult to see him at work. I had a hard time controlling my emotions. I cried and cried. Even though he tried to comfort me, I wanted no part of his sympathy. I nevertheless did relent to meet with him because I wanted to talk about his lying, betrayal, and infidelity.

By this time, it was weeks away from graduation. He was planning to go to college nearby, and I was planning to pursue a career in radiology as an X-ray technician at a local hospital. I was clear that I did not want to get back together with someone who wasn't honest and would cheat on me, but I wanted to know why. Why did he feel the need to thoughtlessly break my heart?

And yet, on some level, I didn't want to know.

We met Saturday after work at the park. My heart was in my throat. I could barely say, "I'm not responsible for what happened—you are. What were you thinking?"

He began by saying, "I'm sorry for lying and cheating on you. I was a total jerk. You didn't deserve that. Can we still be friends? How can I make it up to you?"

I said, "Friends? I don't think so. You chose her! There's NOTHING you can do to make it up to me, but I do accept your apology."

While writing this book, I recalled this experience, applied the process to open my heart, and was able to embrace the wonderful love-at-first-sight memories we shared and heal the indelicate way our relationship ended.

Final Thoughts

It's never too late to heal your relationships with your intimate partners. For those whose partners are still living, it could be interesting to see what naturally happens in those relationships. Now that you've begun the process of healing relationships with your partner(s)—and the past is in the past where it belongs—don't be surprised if they reach out to you. Should there be anything left for you to say when they contact you, go ahead and communicate from your heart. No matter how the conversation ends up, it'll be more complete than before you began the **Healing Process.**

I predict your relationship with your partner, or future partners, will hold more intimacy, fun, adventure, passion, joy, and love from doing this healing.

Remember to do something special for yourself as acknowledgment for the courage it took to heal the past with your intimate partner(s) and welcome—with an open heart—a magical life of loving and being loved.

6

Healing Your Relationships with Your Immediate Family

*"Brothers and sisters are special. They fight. They make up.
They laugh. They cry. They're far from perfect.
But when you really need them, they have your back."*
~Helen M. Barry

After your parents and intimate partners, the next group with which to heal hurtful experiences is your immediate family. In this chapter, I've defined immediate family as your children and siblings. This includes biological relationships, step-relationships, adoptive relationships, foster relationships, grandchildren, and godchildren. When I refer to your child or your sibling, it includes all these categories.

For those of you who are an only child—or have no children in any of the categories listed above—you can go to the next chapter, *Healing with Your Extended Family*.

Children can say or do harmful things—often unintentionally—that hurt you in ways you never knew you could be hurt. When your 4-year-old son shouts, *"I hate you,"* because you won't let him eat candy before dinner, you know in your head that he doesn't mean that—but it still hurts your heart. When your teenager rejects everything you say and/or do every day, you may know it's part of growing up—but it still hurts your heart. When your adult daughter refuses to travel home for Thanksgiving, you may know she's doing what she needs to do—but it still hurts your heart.

To your children, your harsh actions, reactions, and responses to what's of interest and importance to them—like, *"No, you can't have a pony!"*—can cause actual harm throughout their life. Even though it may seem insignificant to you at the time—it may have real significance for them.

When you're growing up, your siblings can be your closest friends or so much older that they can't identify with you or your life. As you all grow older and your lives diverge—differences of opinion, lifestyle, religious belief, socio-economic status—often cause rifts in your relationships, more so than distance and age. In any case—because they're your siblings—you can be deeply hurt by their words or actions in much the same way as you can deeply hurt them with yours.

Now's the time to heal all the hurts that have been affecting the quality of your relationships with your children and siblings.

This is a visualization process, and I know it may feel strange to imagine your children—especially when they are very young—receiving and saying the **Healing Process** statements. Remember this is a visualization, so I recommend just going with it.

It's time to heal your relationships with your immediate family. As you heal each experience with your child or sibling, notice how you feel. You may feel lighter in spirit and more free to be yourself. You may also notice that many areas of your life begin to open up and become easier. Remember to schedule time regularly until you have healed all the hurtful experiences with your immediate family and feel peace within.

Healing Process with Your Immediate Family

Get out your *Healing Notebook*. Create a separate page for each child or sibling in your life. Choose the relationship you want to heal before you begin your session. Set aside the time you need. Find a quiet place where you won't be disturbed and get comfortable. Close your eyes and center yourself in the present moment by taking a few deep breaths through your nose.

Healing Harm Your Immediate Family Caused You

Recall and Record

RECALL the first time you were rejected, dishonored, humiliated, insulted, etc., by the child or sibling who harmed you. Whether they said, *"I am sorry"* or not, the harm was done.

RECORD what happened, their name and relationship to you, your ages, and how the experience made you feel.

Release Your Feelings

Allow the emotions to surface and as each feeling comes up, do the work to release it.

Free Yourself from the Harm

It's time now to energetically free yourself from the harm associated with the experience. Close your eyes and visualize the child or sibling standing in front of you. Say the following statement aloud:

"I'm giving you back the responsibility I've been assuming for the harm you caused me. By giving you back your responsibility, I'm also giving you back your dignity. I know you have the strength to carry it. Please, give me your blessings as I direct my energy and attention—which are now free—to create my magical life."

Visualize the child or sibling gladly receive your communication and imagine them saying to you—with honor and respect:

"It's no longer necessary for you to assume my responsibility for the harm I caused you and I accept the guilt for my behavior. I give you my blessings as you move forward in your life."

Receive an Authentic Apology

FIRST: Imagine your child or sibling genuinely saying, *"I am sorry for _____ (what I said or didn't say; did or didn't do)."*

THEN: Imagine them saying what positive actions they will take to ensure the harmful behavior won't occur again.

FINALLY: Imagine your child or sibling asking, *"How can I make it up to you and restore our relationship?"* Picture what you need and visualize them doing it. Allow yourself to accept your child's or sibling's blessings.

Healing Harm You Caused Your Immediate Family

Recall and Record

RECALL the first time you caused harm to a child or sibling. Whether you said, *"I am sorry"* or not, the harm was done.

RECORD what happened, their name and relationship to you, your ages, and what feelings you inflicted on them.

Release Your Feelings

Allow the emotions to surface and as each feeling comes up, do the work to release it.

Take Back the Responsibility and Guilt

It's time now to energetically free yourself from the harm associated with the experience. Close your eyes and visualize the child or sibling standing in front of you. Say the following statement aloud:

> *"I take back the responsibility and accept the guilt for the harm I caused you. It is no longer necessary for you to assume this responsibility. I give you my blessings as you move forward in your life."*

Visualize the child or sibling gladly receive your communication and imagine them saying to you—with honor and respect:

> *"I appreciate the generosity and courage it took for you to admit that your unkind behavior offended me deeply."*

Offer an Authentic Apology

FIRST: Sincerely say, *"I am sorry for _____ (what I said or didn't say; did or didn't do)."*

THEN: Imagine telling the child or sibling what positive actions you will take to ensure the harmful behavior won't occur again.

FINALLY: Imagine asking your child or sibling, *"How can I make it up to you and restore our relationship?"* Picture them telling you what they need—then you COMPLYING. Imagine your child or sibling accepting your blessings.

Embrace the Healing—You to Your Child or Sibling, Your Child or Sibling to You

When you consider there are many, many reasons (e.g. judgmental, being inconsiderate and disrespectful, stubborn, contempt, jealousy, aggressive, pessimistic, etc.)—which are not necessarily intentional—that explain a person's hurtful reactions and behaviors, you can begin to have compassion and forgiveness for yourself and others.

Integration is the key to healing. To assimilate all of the energetic renewal available, always allocate an adequate amount of time after healing the harm from each experience. Sit quietly, breathe deeply through your nose—which will help you to relax—breathe in love and breathe out any tension that you may be holding in your body.

Notice and feel the love you now have for your child or sibling. Allow it into all the cells of your body. Let it permeate your whole being.

Feel free to write in your *Healing Notebook* about your experience of using the **Healing Process**—how you feel now, plus any actions you feel inspired to take.

My Healing Journey with My Siblings

I am the oldest of four children. My mother and I live in Phoenix, Arizona, about 35 miles from one another. My three younger siblings are spread out from Wisconsin to Wyoming.

As my mother aged, she developed some medical and cognitive issues that required more and more personal care. The expectation was assumed—among my siblings—that it was my responsibility to make sure that all her needs were met because I was the one living closest to her.

I was working full-time in my own business—in addition to traveling across town 90 minutes round trip three times per week—to help mom maintain her rapidly declining independence. I was paying her bills, taking her to doctor's appointments, doing laundry and light housekeeping chores—for her and her two cats—plus tackling a variety of small home improvement projects and so much more.

From childhood, my mother and I alway seemed to be at odds with one another, and as her dementia progressed, it strained our relationship even more. No matter what I said or did for her, I received little to no appreciation or praise from my mother, AND—for that matter—no financial support or encouragement from my siblings. The overwhelming feeling that nobody cared hung over me for years.

To add insult to injury, my husband was diagnosed with an aggressive form of cancer, and managing his care, in addition to that of my mother, took a toll on my business. I became so desperate for help I demanded that my brother take on the responsibility of being my mother's Healthcare Power of Attorney thinking that it would inspire him to get involved. It made no difference. I was still expected to be an advocate for her and her primary family contact.

My bitterness and resentment intensified after each passing week as I was putting everyone's life before my needs, and it was starting to affect my well-being. I was losing weight rapidly. I was having difficulty sleeping and accomplishing routine tasks.

After my husband passed away—and with him, his income—I was struggling financially. I urgently needed a reasonable sum of money to pay a few bills. With great trepidation, I set up a conference call with my siblings and asked to be compensated—from mom's bank account—for all the time and effort I had been providing to our mother's care out of the goodness of my heart. I implored them to consider that it was worthy of compensation since it took productive time away from my business and prevented me from participating in my personal activities and interests with friends.

Without hesitating, my brother and youngest sister both said, "Yes." Then, my other sister unequivocally said, "No, that's Mom's money. You can borrow it for this month, but you will have to pay her back." Her words devastated me, so much so, that I could barely speak. But, what happened next hurt me so deeply it infuriated me. Neither my brother nor sister—who had first generously agreed—stood up for me. They simply acquiesced to her emphatic refusal.

In my stunned silence, I faintly heard them say that they appreciated all the things I did for mom. These words sounded hollow. They had the perfect opportunity to honor my sacrifice and demonstrate their gratitude but chose instead to be less than charitable. It wasn't even their money. My mom had more than enough to cover her needs.

Needless to say, I didn't speak to any of them for quite some time. Furthermore, they felt no need to call and see how I was doing—which was even more hurtful.

Everything changed when the inevitable day came that mom had a delusional episode and was no longer safe to stay in her home alone. In an emergency intervention, along with my mom's doctor and authorization from my brother in Wisconsin, *we determined that it was necessary to immediately transport my mom to a conveniently-located assisted living facility near my home and enrolled her in hospice care.*

Mom was utterly confused, irate, indignant, demanding, behaving aggressively toward me and the staff, and could not or would not be comforted. I was heartbroken to have to be the one to leave her there in that condition.

Once mom was settled, it was time to find her cats a new home, donate her clothing and household items, box up sentimental heirlooms, and liquidate her car, furniture, appliances, and mobile home.

Thankfully, my brother, as well as my oldest sister and her husband, flew in to help me accomplish the monumental endeavor in just five days. After they left, my youngest sister flew in to help organize all the boxes that were hauled and stacked haphazardly in my garage. It was heartwarming to see my siblings come together to honor the things of value that were revered by our mother.

It felt so good to be surrounded by family, even though my siblings only stayed for a short time. I had forgotten how much they meant to me and how I am still—and always will be—connected to them. I also realized I was still harboring animosity toward their lack of support, inconsideration, and unrealistic expectations.

Since all of my sibling were unable to be here with me, I chose to energetically release and heal the harm they caused me.

Knowing that one's mind doesn't know the difference between what's real and what's imaginary made it possible for me to visualize my sisters and brother—as if they are physically standing in front of me—saying, "We're sorry for not putting ourselves in your shoes and granting you the compensation you deserved. We're ready to do that now. Please, let us know what works for you." Then I visualized my sister who had denied me compensation, ask, "How can we make it up to you?"

The thought that they could make it up to me and remove completely all the harm and all the hurt feelings, made me so, so happy. I could feel them honoring my contribution to our mother, acknowledging me for my sacrifices, and in unison all agreeing that it WAS truly worthy of significant compensation.

After accepting their authentic amends, I integrated their acknowledgment by doing something extra special for myself with my friends, making it possible for me to maintain a healthy long-distance relationship with all of my siblings.

Final Thoughts

This process, in ***this*** chapter, in ***this*** book provides the possibility of renewed relationships with deeper levels of understanding, acceptance, respect, compassion, and love—with your immediate family.

For those who chose a child or sibling who is still living, it could be interesting to see what naturally happens in your relationship. Now that you've begun the process of healing relationships with your immediate family—and the past is in the past where it belongs—don't be surprised if they reach out to you. Should there be anything left for you to say when they contact you, go ahead and communicate from your heart. No matter how the conversation ends up, it'll be more complete than before you began the **Healing Process.**

I predict relationships with those in your immediate family, will hold more love, adventure, happiness, and fun from doing this healing.

Remember to do something special for yourself as acknowledgment for the courage it took to heal the past with your child or sibling and welcome—with an open heart—a magical life together.

Healing Your Relationships with Your Extended Family

"The way you help heal the world is you start with your own family."
~ Mother Teresa

Now that you have healed the majority of the hurtful experiences with your parents, your partners, your children, and your siblings, you are ready to continue the **Healing Process** with the rest of your family. I recommend including grandparents, aunts, uncles, cousins, in-laws, step families, blended families, best friends, etc.—everyone you consider to be part of your extended family. When I refer to your extended family member, all these categories are included.

It's time to heal your relationships with your extended family. As you heal experience after experience with each family member, notice how you feel. You may feel lighter in spirit and more free to be yourself. You may also notice that many areas of your life begin to open up and become easier. Remember to schedule time regularly until you have healed all the hurtful experiences with extended family members and feel peace within.

Healing Process with Your Extended Family

Get out your *Healing Notebook*. Create a separate page for each extended family member. Choose the relationship you want to heal before you begin your session. Set aside the time you need. Find a quiet place where you won't be disturbed and get comfortable. Close your eyes and center yourself in the present moment by taking a few deep breaths through your nose.

Healing Harm Your Extended Family Caused You

Recall and Record

RECALL the first time you were punished, ridiculed, humiliated, frightened, etc., by an extended family member who harmed you. Whether they said, *"I am sorry"* or not, the harm was done.

RECORD what happened, their name and relationship to you, your ages, and how the experience made you feel.

Release Your Feelings

Allow the emotions to surface and as each feeling comes up, do the work to release it.

Free Yourself from the Harm

It's time now to energetically free yourself from the harm associated with the experience. Close your eyes and visualize the extended family member standing in front of you. Say aloud the following:

"I'm giving you back the responsibility I've been assuming for the harm you caused me. By giving you back your responsibility, I'm also giving you back your dignity. I know you have the strength to carry it. Please, give me your blessings as I direct my energy and attention—which are now free—to create my magical life."

Visualize the extended family member gladly receive your communication and imagine them saying to you—with honor and respect:

"It's no longer necessary for you to assume my responsibility for the harm I caused you and I accept the guilt for my behavior. I give you my blessings as you move forward in your life."

Receive an Authentic Apology

FIRST: Imagine your extended family member genuinely saying, *"I am sorry for _____ (what I said or didn't say; did or didn't do)."*

THEN: Imagine them saying what positive actions they will take to ensure the harmful behavior won't occur again.

FINALLY: Imagine your extended family member asking, *"How can I make it up to you and restore our relationship?"* Picture what you need and visualize them doing it. Allow yourself to accept your extended family member's blessings.

Healing Harm You Caused Your Extended Family

Recall and Record

RECALL the first time you caused harm to an extended family member. Whether you said, *"I am sorry"* or not, the harm was done. RECORD what happened, their name and relationship to you, your ages, and what feelings you inflicted on them.

Release Your Feelings

Allow the emotions to surface and as each feeling comes up, do the work to release it.

Take Back the Responsibility and Guilt

It's time now to energetically free yourself from the harm associated with the experience. Close your eyes and visualize the extended family member standing in front of you. Say aloud the following:

> *"I take back the responsibility and accept the guilt for the harm I caused you. It is no longer necessary for you to assume this responsibility. I give you my blessings as you move forward in your life."*

Visualize the extended family member gladly receive your communication and imagine them saying to you—with honor and respect:

> *"I appreciate the generosity and courage it took for you to admit that your unkind behavior offended me deeply."*

Offer an Authentic Apology

FIRST: Sincerely say, *"I am sorry for _____ (what I said or didn't say; did or didn't do)."*

THEN: Imagine telling the extended family member what positive actions you will take to ensure the harmful behavior won't occur again. FINALLY: Imagine asking your extended family member, *"How can I make it up to you and restore our relationship?"* Picture them telling you what they need—then you COMPLYING. Imagine your extended family member accepting your blessings.

Embrace the Healing—You to Your Extended Family Member, Your Extended Family Member to You

When you consider there are many, many reasons (e.g. frustration, regret, insecurity, resentment, envy, blame, etc.)—which are not necessarily intentional—that explain a person's hurtful reactions and behaviors, you can begin to have compassion and forgiveness for yourself and others.

Integration is the key to healing. To assimilate all of the energetic renewal available, always allocate an adequate amount of time after healing the harm from each experience. Sit quietly, breathe deeply through your nose—which will help you to relax—breathe in love and breathe out any tension that you may be holding in your body.

Notice and feel the appreciation you now have for your extended family member. Allow it into all the cells of your body. Let it permeate your whole being.

Feel free to write in your *Healing Notebook* about your experience of using the **Healing Process**—how you feel now, plus any actions you feel inspired to take.

My Healing Journey with an Extended Family Member

Of all my relatives, I am closest to my father's youngest brother, Uncle Jim, and his second wife, Aunt Lynn. They were close to my age, and whenever they traveled from San Jose to Milwaukee to visit my dad, I would always drive up from

Chicago to spend time with them. We had a lot in common and enjoyed each other's company. We kept in touch by phone every few months, and after I moved to Phoenix, we got to see each other about every two years over the course of ten years.

When I had the opportunity to visit with Uncle Jim and Aunt Lynn, it was an added bonus to get to see my cousins, Drew and Brett, on the rare occasions that they also happened to be in town.

During one phone conversation about two and a half years ago, my aunt and uncle announced that my cousin, Brett, was getting married in Las Vegas. They told me I would be getting an invitation and they hoped I could come. I told them I'd do my best to be there.

When the invitation arrived three months later, I realized, due to some unexpected expenses after my husband's death, that I couldn't justify spending the money for the trip. I was so embarrassed about my financial situation, I couldn't get my fingers to the phone to tell them, so I returned the R.S.V.P. card just before the deadline, and checked off that I wasn't coming. Brett and I weren't even very close, so I didn't see how my attendance would make much difference. I did however, send a wedding card with a respectable gift of money included.

Mid November, a couple of weeks before the wedding, my aunt made it a point to call me to let me know she and my uncle were very disappointed that I couldn't make it. They had so been looking forward to seeing me and expected me to be there.

Guilt set in. I was not feeling very good about myself. I thought, "I should've made arrangements to go and just charged everything." I went on and on in my mind, justifying my reasons for not going to try to make myself feel better. I kept replaying—over and over and over again—my Aunt Lynn saying how disappointed they were with my decision.

As time passed, I justified my behavior and came to believe that I had done the very best I could do and forgave myself.

About six months after Brett's wedding, I was in California attending a dance camp with my boyfriend, and had an opportunity to visit my aunt and uncle. I was really looking forward to seeing them again—I had forgotten all about the wedding situation.

I was shocked when the first thing out of my uncle's mouth was, "Brett was so hurt that you didn't come to his wedding last December. He hasn't quite gotten over it!"

I responded, "I didn't think my presence really meant that much to him. We're not that close. I didn't have the money and was too embarrassed to say so."

My uncle told me, "Well, he was really upset that you didn't make more of an effort to come—and so were we."

I said, "I'm sorry, Uncle Jim, I'll call Brett and apologize," to which he didn't say a thing and abruptly stormed out the room. However, about ten minutes later, he came back and started berating me again for failing to beg, borrow, or steal the money necessary to attend the wedding. After all, how much could it cost? The tension between us was palpable.

While he was scolding me, I was sure he was thinking, "You have money to take a trip to California for a week, but you couldn't come to our son's wedding?" With that assumption in mind, my shame compelled me to tell him, "In my defense, I'm only able to visit you today because my boyfriend is paying for most of this trip." It didn't seem to phase him one little bit.

By this time, I was really feeling guilty and worthless—and frankly, I just wanted to leave. I knew in my heart though that leaving wasn't the answer. I took a deep breath, calmed down, looked right into my uncle's eyes, and with tears in mine said,

"I am so sorry that I disappointed and hurt you, Aunt Lynn, and Brett. I regret the choice I made. I will never do it again. Next time I receive a wedding invitation, I'll honor the love expressed by the request, and make every effort to attend. Can you find it in your heart to forgive me?" He hugged me and with great tenderness said, *"I forgive you. Remember to apologize to your Aunt and Brett."*

Uncle Jim and I still enjoy talking on the phone every few months. We discuss everything from my passion to write and my upcoming book, the progress and frustration of their home renovations, and current health concerns. I'm so thankful for the opportunity to connect to a little piece of my late father, when I talk to my uncle.

Final Thoughts

Healing hurt feelings with extended family members can have a ripple effect on all members of your family, even those who may never participate in this process. Expect to feel deeper connections, experience more love, and express sincere gratitude for your family members.

For those who chose an extended family member who is still living, it could be interesting to see what naturally happens in your relationship. Now that you've begun the process of healing relationships with your extended family—and the past is in the past where it belongs—don't be surprised if they reach out to you. Should there be anything left for you to say when they contact you, go ahead and communicate from your heart. No matter how the conversation ends up, it'll be more complete than before you began the **Healing Process.**

Remember to do something special for yourself as acknowledgment for the courage it took to heal the past with your extended family members and welcome compassion and understanding into your ever-expanding magical life.

Healing Your Relationships with People in Your Community

"It's not an easy journey to get to a place where you forgive people. But it is such a powerful place, because it frees you."
~ Tyler Perry

Now that you have healed the majority of the hurtful experiences with your closest relationships, you are ready to move on to include the other influential people in your life that you knew:

- at home—your friends, family friends, babysitters
- at school—other students, kids on the playground, schoolyard bullies, teachers, coaches
- in your neighborhood—neighbors, clergy, club and scout leaders, librarians
- in the wider world—doctors, nurses, landlords, social media contacts.

NOTE: Chapter 9 will be the opportunity to heal with people at work.

Be sure to include any hurtful experiences from the time when you were growing up until the present. To free yourself to create a magical life, don't leave anyone or anything out. When an incident comes to mind, even though it may seem like something small, include it.

You may want to modify this process slightly to include a series of people, as I did in *My Healing Journey with Community Members*, at the end of this chapter. Each of the five people expressed a similar hurtful behavior and revealed a pattern that I thought would be beneficial to share.

It's time to heal your relationships with the people in your community. As you heal each experience, notice how you feel. You may feel lighter in spirit and more free to be yourself. You may also notice that many areas of your life begin to open up and become easier. Remember to schedule time regularly until you have healed all the incidents with your community members and feel peace within.

Healing Process with Community Members

Get out your *Healing Notebook*. Create a separate page for each community member. Choose the relationship you want to heal before you begin your session. Set aside the time you need. Find a quiet place where you won't be disturbed and get comfortable. Close your eyes and center yourself in the present moment by taking a few deep breaths through your nose.

Healing Harm Your Community Members Caused You

> *Recall and Record*
> RECALL the first time you felt powerless, overwhelmed, shamed, violated, etc., by a community member who harmed you. Whether they said, *"I am sorry"* or not, the harm was done.
> RECORD what happened, their name and relationship to you, your ages, and how the experience made you feel.
>
> *Release Your Feelings*
> Allow the emotions to surface and as each feeling comes up, do the work to release it.
>
> *Free Yourself from the Harm*
> It's time now to energetically free yourself from the harm associated with the experience. Close your eyes and visualize the community member standing in front of you. Say aloud the following:

> "I'm giving you back the responsibility I've been assuming for the harm you caused me. By giving you back your responsibility, I'm also giving you back your dignity. I know you have the strength to carry it. Please, give me your blessings as I direct my energy and attention—which are now free—to create my magical life."

Visualize the community member gladly receive your communication and imagine them saying to you—with honor and respect:

> "It's no longer necessary for you to assume my responsibility for the harm I caused you and I accept the guilt for my behavior. I give you my blessings as you move forward in your life."

Receive an Authentic Apology

FIRST: Imagine your community member genuinely saying, *"I am sorry for _____ (what I said or didn't say; did or didn't do)."*

THEN: Imagine them saying what positive actions they will take to ensure the harmful behavior won't occur again.

FINALLY: Imagine your community member asking, *"How can I make it up to you and restore our relationship?"* Picture what you need and visualize them doing it. Allow yourself to accept your community member's blessings.

Healing Harm You Caused Your Community Members

Recall and Record

RECALL the first time you caused harm to a community member. Whether you said, *"I am sorry"* or not, the harm was done.

RECORD what happened, their name and relationship to you, your ages, and what feelings you inflicted on them.

Release Your Feelings
Allow the emotions to surface and as each feeling comes up, do the work to release it.

Take Back the Responsibility and Guilt
It's time now to energetically free yourself from the harm associated with the experience. Close your eyes and visualize the community member standing in front of you. Say aloud the following:
"I take back the responsibility and accept the guilt for the harm I caused you. It is no longer necessary for you to assume this responsibility. I give you my blessings as you move forward in your life."
Visualize the community member gladly receive your communication and imagine them saying to you—with honor and respect:
"I appreciate the generosity and courage it took for you to admit that your unkind behavior offended me deeply."

Offer an Authentic Apology
FIRST: Sincerely say, *"I am sorry for* _____ *(what I said or didn't say; did or didn't do)."*
THEN: Imagine telling the community member what positive actions you will take to ensure the harmful behavior won't occur again.
FINALLY: Imagine asking your community member, *"How can I make it up to you and restore our relationship?"* Picture them telling you what they need—then you COMPLYING. Imagine your community member accepting your blessings.

Embrace the Healing—You to Your Community Member, Your Community Member to You

When you consider there are many, many reasons (e.g. gossip, addictions, intimidation, intolerance, negative outlook, paranoia, mistrust, hatred, etc.)

—which are not necessarily intentional—that explain a person's hurtful reactions and behaviors, you can begin to have compassion and forgiveness for yourself and others.

Integration is the key to healing. To assimilate all of the energetic renewal available, always allocate an adequate amount of time after healing the harm from each experience. Sit quietly, breathe deeply through your nose—which will help you to relax—breathe in love and breathe out any tension that you may be holding in your body.

Notice and feel the appreciation you now have for your community member. Allow it into all the cells of your body. Let it permeate your whole being.

Feel free to write in your *Healing Notebook* about your experience of using the **Healing Process**—how you feel now, plus any actions you feel inspired to take.

My Healing Journey with Community Members

In January of every year, I take an inventory of my life and my relationships. This year, I used my Healing Notebook to recall and record hurtful experiences with people in my community.

I listed the names of five people I once considered friends. It occurred to me that each friendship ended with experiences that were all too similar.

As I wrote down what happened with each relationship, a pattern began to emerge. Interestingly, each friend abruptly ended our relationship—out of the blue—without so much as an explanation. And, to this day I still have no idea why.

I was committed to healing what happened with each friend, and the rejection I experienced from each, and then continue on to reveal and heal the origin of the pattern. First, let me tell you a little about each friend and what happened.

Sue. *We met while attending Alison Armstrong's Understanding Men, Celebrating Women workshop. We were talking weekly, by phone, openly sharing what was going on with the men in our* lives and exchanging feedback. We were inspiring each other to remember what we had learned in the workshop. We both signed up for a second workshop in California and decided to share a hotel room, to cut down on expenses. Since Sue was flying in, I drove over from Phoenix with a couple of coolers of food for both of us. We spent the week together enjoying each other's company.

I noticed that Sue was a get up, get ready, and get out the door kind of gal—and I'm not. I really enjoy taking my time in the morning.

One morning, when I had just gotten up, Sue announced she wanted to leave in ten minutes. I got ready as quickly as I could. However, I needed to wash my hair, so it was almost an hour before I was ready. I knew she was upset, and I could feel her frustration, but I really couldn't—with a moment's notice—make it work for both of us.

I respectfully requested, "In the future, please let me know what your plans are, so I can accommodate your needs and still stay true to myself." Without further discussion, I drove us to the workshop and picked up coffee on the way. The rest of our time together at the workshop went well. I assumed the incident was resolved.

After returning home from the workshop, we were both very busy and didn't talk for a couple of weeks. When Sue called me, the first thing she said was, "I no longer want to be friends with you." She didn't give me any reason, she just said, "I don't want to talk about it or tell you what's going on. I simply need to pull away and no longer engage with you." I was stunned!

Wow. No explanation! I hung up the phone in tears. My mind was racing—what did I say or do to deserve this? What could I have possibly done to cause this? Since she wouldn't tell me anything, I assumed it was because her expectations were not met on that fateful morning in California.

Rebecca. We met through mutual friends who had mutual interests. Rebecca and I began hanging out together every month or so, sharing—practitioner to practitioner—our different healing methods. Rebecca had expertise in Native American ceremonies which intrigued me. Although she was quite a bit younger than I, she was exceptionally wise for her years.

Rebecca asked me to mentor her in the five healing methods I was proficient at, in exchange for therapeutic massages from her. She was curious about all of them and wanted to learn about each one. We got together for a coaching session within a week. She was particularly interested in Resonance Repatterning® so I gave her some of my old books to review and we scheduled another session in two weeks.

When she called for her coaching session, she told me she had broken her foot, and let me know that she needed time to herself to heal and get ready to move to a new home. She requested to suspend our mentoring sessions for the time being and I agreed.

I waited a couple of weeks and reached out to her as a friend, just to see how she was doing and to ask if she needed any help moving. She didn't return my voicemail until a month later.

That call was fraught with emotion and her tone was harsh. She was very angry and told me, "You betrayed my trust and I no longer want to have anything to do with you!"

I asked her, "What are you talking about? What did I say or do that offended you?"

She responded, "I don't want to talk about it!"

I asked, "How can I apologize for something when I don't even know what happened? Please tell me what's going on."

She again refused to tell me.

I told her, "Rebecca, I would never intentionally do or say anything to harm you. I care about you."

She still wouldn't tell me, so I said, "OK, if you ever want to talk about it, just call. Have a great life."

We both hung up. I still have no idea what happened. I assumed one of our mutual friends said something insensitive implicating me and a misunderstanding ensued.

Anton. I met Anton at a dance lesson. I was fascinated by his accent and his eastern European culture. During the four months we were dating, I came to realize that he wanted me to behave in ways that were inconsistent with my true nature. He expected me to eat what he thought I should eat—including things I told him were detrimental to my health; to spend less time with my friends; to stop social activities he didn't want to participate in; to wear what he thought I should wear; to always watch movies he wanted to watch; it even got down to what time of day I was supposed to take a shower.

I stopped dating him, although we managed to remain friends, which was working just fine for both of us. We still danced together weekly at the dance studio and saw each other at other social events.

The holidays were coming and he was scheduled to have major surgery. I called him a few days before his surgery—here's how the conversation went:

I asked, "Do you want me to take you to the hospital?"
"No."
"Do you want me to come to the hospital to visit you?"
"No."
"Do you want me to pick up your son, who's flying in tomorrow?"
"No."
"Do you want to get together for Christmas?"
"No. I have to go now."

"So, this is all you have to say?"

"Yes."

"You're not going to tell me what's going on?"

"No."

"OK then. Thanks for the memories. Hope your surgery goes well."

"OK."

WOW! Again—goodbye, so long, adios, sayonara, arrivederci—dropped like a hot potato with no explanation. I can only assume that our relationship wasn't worth pursuing because he couldn't change me to meet his needs and desires.

Kyle. Kyle is also someone I met on the dance floor. The night we met he asked me to dance to five songs in a row. It was highly unusual, but I liked it, I loved it, I wanted some more of it. A couple of weeks later, while we were dancing cheek to cheek, he asked me to go out to dinner and to the theatre. I said, "Yes." I didn't know for sure if it was a date, so I offered to pay for my meal. He said he'd get it.

For about eight months, we continued going dancing, out to the theater, and traveling together to attend dance camps in nearby states.

Kyle was someone who needed to share his knowledge. He talked incessantly about everything under the sun, from the local flora and fauna to the entire history of the cities we went to where we participated in dance camps. It was never-ending, so much so, that I could barely travel 20 minutes in a car with him. Yet he rarely talked about himself or his feelings. I shared my concerns with him about his behavior and he told me he had heard that from other women as well.

The way in which Kyle expressed his affection was to shower me constantly with knickknacks. When he started talking about our future as, "romantic RV dance gypsies roaming the country together," I came to believe that he was more interested in a long-term relationship than I was. I just wasn't "in love" with him and told him so. We talked about it and decided to remain friends and still go dancing and occasionally to the theatre, which is all I really wanted anyway.

Suddenly, he stopped returning my phone calls and texts. It quickly became apparent that he didn't want to continue our friendship at all—when in fact he seemed so eager to do so.

Holy smokes! This one caught me by surprise. It took me awhile to get over losing Kyle as a friend. I assumed that because he couldn't talk about his feelings, any long-term relationship with ANY woman would be doomed.

Martin. It had been two years since my beloved husband liberated his soul from his physical body when I told God I was finally ready to attract a wonderful loving partner again. Within a few days, one of my best friends called with an incredible opportunity to participate in Dr. Joe Dispenza's meditation retreat in Cancun with her. I jumped at the chance to go. One of the requirements was to create a mind movie video with all the things I wanted in my life. The possibility occurred to me that I could meet my new husband at this event. Why not?

The event attracted 1,100 people from all over the world. On the third day, I met Martin. We hit it off right away. We had a lot in common and similar spiritual interests. Could HE be THE ONE? But, since I lived in Phoenix, AZ and he lived in Vancouver, BC, the chances of something working out were slim to none.

After the retreat, we went our separate ways, although we talked frequently. Not more than a month later—on the same weekend that my friend, Sally, and her boyfriend flew in from

Santa Fe—Martin came to visit me. The four of us had an absolute blast together laughing, dancing, and seeing the sights of Phoenix, in addition to lounging in the backyard, drinking Cabernet Sauvignon and barbecuing steaks!

After Martin returned home, we continued to talk daily—sometimes until the wee hours of the morning. The conversations were rich and rewarding. The pillow talk was great. In one of our phone conversations, Martin told me that our friendship meant a lot to him—even more important than being lovers or potential partners. We also talked about me visiting Vancouver in the summer and him returning to Phoenix in the winter. My hopes were high—could he actually be THE ONE?

As long distant relationships go, the calls from him gradually tapered off, and then nothing—dead silence—not a word.

I was heartbroken. I really liked who he was and who we were together. I assumed that he got cold feet, lost interest, or needed companionship a little closer to home.

I guess the probability of meeting my new husband at the retreat was not meant to be.

The Pattern. Once I had written down these experiences, I became present to all the emotions: confusion, betrayal, devastation, sadness, and anger. I allowed myself to feel—REALLY feel—each one and release them as they arose.

Since I still have no clue why each friend behaved in such a hurtful manner, AND I initially assumed THEY were to blame, I followed the healing process for those I believed caused me harm. But, inasmuch as I could have unknowingly caused them harm, I followed the process to heal any offense I may have caused them.

I spent a lot of time integrating all the forgiveness and amends until I could finally feel myself releasing the tension

I was holding in my body. Assimilating the energetic renewal that became available from the experience of healing the same behavior of five people, was euphoric.

I felt profoundly free to receive their blessings and direct my energy and attention toward creating my magical life complete with honor, respect, love, and honest communication.

When this healing was complete, all I wanted to do was surround myself with friends who loved me. So, I invited five girlfriends to join me at the day spa for a full day of pampering. Some got a massage, others got a mani-pedi, I got a facial and we all went out for dinner and drinks to celebrate.

This deep dive into relationships with community members revealed a pattern of people dear to me abruptly leaving without an explanation. It occurred to me that this pattern originated when my father left—without an explanation—when I was 12, which I wrote about in Chapter 4.

Final Thoughts

Healing with people in your community who impacted you from childhood to the present gives you the freedom to be yourself—fully self-expressed and able to speak your truth to others. It gives you the capacity to expand and accept others just the way they are, and actively participate in activities with others you previously avoided.

For those who chose a community member who is still living, it could be interesting to see what naturally happens in your relationship. Now that you've begun the process of healing relationships with your community members—and the past is in the past where it belongs—don't be surprised if they reach out to you. Should there be anything left for you to say when they contact you, go ahead and communicate from your heart. No matter how the conversation ends up, it'll be more complete than before you began the **Healing Process.**

Remember to do something special for yourself as acknowledgment for the courage it took to heal the past with your community members. Always and forever appreciate your endurance and determination to create your magical life.

9

Healing Your Relationships with People at Work

"When employees respect each other and get along in the workplace, it's amazing how productivity increases, morale increases and employees are more courteous to customers."
~ Maureen Wild

Now that you've healed most of the hurtful experiences with your closest relationships and the influential people in your life, it's time to move on to include the people at work.

Most of us spend more time working than at home, unless of course, we have a home office. In this chapter, you will be applying the **Healing Process** to your work relationships, including: your boss, your co-workers, your subordinates, your clients, and vendors, etc. When I refer to your co-workers, it encompasses all these categories.

Meaningful work and job satisfaction seem to go hand in hand. Here are some statistics I thought might interest you. Several studies over the past few years on job satisfaction in America has shown: only 45% of workers say they are either satisfied or extremely satisfied with their jobs; 85% of employees are indifferent to the organization for which they work and give their time, but not their best effort, creating approximately $7 trillion in lost productivity; and 69% of them say they'd work harder if they were better appreciated. Why?

Could it be because interpersonal relationships at work need to be healed?

Imagine a workplace where everyone comes to work feeling happy, fulfilled, and ready to succeed—from the CEO to the bosses to the workers.

Healing the workplace starts with you—one work environment at a time—including babysitting, your paper route, helping out on the family farm, waiting tables to pay for college, internships, working in a large corporation, owning your own business—whatever you deem to be work.

It's time to heal your work relationships. As you heal each experience with your co-workers, notice how you feel. You may feel lighter in spirit and more free to be yourself. You may also notice that many areas of your life begin to open up and become easier. Remember to schedule time regularly until you have healed all the incidents with your co-workers and feel peace within.

Healing Process with the People at Work

Get out your *Healing Notebook*. Create a separate page for each co-worker. Choose the relationship you want to heal before you begin your session. Set aside the time you need. Find a quiet place where you won't be disturbed and get comfortable. Close your eyes and center yourself in the present moment by taking a few deep breaths through your nose.

Healing Harm Your Co-Workers Caused You

> *Recall and Record*
> RECALL the first time you felt powerless, overwhelmed, shamed, violated, etc., by a co-worker who harmed you. Whether they said, "I am sorry" or not, the harm was done.
> RECORD what happened, their name and relationship to you, your ages, and how the experience made you feel.
>
> *Release Your Feelings*
> Allow the emotions to surface and as each feeling comes up, do the work to release it.

Free Yourself from the Harm

It's time now to energetically free yourself from the harm associated with the experience. Close your eyes and visualize the co-worker standing in front of you. Say the following statement aloud:

"I'm giving you back the responsibility I've been assuming for the harm you caused me. By giving you back your responsibility, I'm also giving you back your dignity. I know you have the strength to carry it. Please, give me your blessings as I direct my energy and attention—which are now free—to create my magical life."

Visualize the co-worker gladly receive your communication and imagine them saying to you—with honor and respect:

"It's no longer necessary for you to assume my responsibility for the harm I caused you and I accept the guilt for my behavior. I give you my blessings as you move forward in your life."

Receive an Authentic Apology

FIRST: Imagine your co-worker genuinely saying, *"I am sorry for _____ (what I said or didn't say; did or didn't do)."*

THEN: Imagine them saying what positive actions they will take to ensure the harmful behavior won't occur again.

FINALLY: Imagine your co-worker asking, *"How can I make it up to you and restore our relationship?"* Picture what you need and visualize them doing it. Allow yourself to accept your co-worker's blessings.

Healing Harm You Caused Your Co-Workers

Recall and Record

RECALL the first time you caused harm to co-worker. Whether you said, *"I am sorry"* or not, the harm was done.

RECORD what happened, their name and relationship to you, your ages, and what feelings you inflicted on them.

Release Your Feelings

Allow the emotions to surface and as each feeling comes up, do the work to release it.

Take Back the Responsibility and Guilt

It's time now to energetically free yourself from the harm associated with the experience. Close your eyes and visualize the co-worker standing in front of you. Say the following statement aloud:

"I take back the responsibility and accept the guilt for the harm I caused you. It is no longer necessary for you to assume this responsibility. I give you my blessings as you move forward in your life."

Visualize the co-worker gladly receive your communication and imagine them saying to you—with honor and respect:

"I appreciate the generosity and courage it took for you to admit that your unkind behavior offended me deeply."

Offer an Authentic Apology

FIRST: Sincerely say, *"I am sorry for _____ (what I said or didn't say; did or didn't do)."*

THEN: Imagine telling the co-worker what positive actions you will take to ensure the harmful behavior won't occur again.

FINALLY: Imagine asking your co-worker, *"How can I make it up to you and restore our relationship?"* Picture them telling you what they need—then you COMPLYING. Imagine your co-worker accepting your blessings.

Embrace the Healing—You to Your Co-Worker, Your Co-Worker to You

When you consider there are many, many reasons (e.g. unhappy home life, overworked, lack of appreciation, gossip, pressure to produce, undermining, passed over for promotions, etc.)—which are not necessarily intentional—that explain a person's hurtful reactions and behaviors, you can begin to have compassion and forgiveness for yourself and others.

Integration is the key to healing. To assimilate all of the energetic renewal available, always allocate an adequate amount of time after healing the harm from each experience. Sit quietly, breathe deeply through your nose—which will help you to relax—breathe in love and breathe out any tension that you may be holding in your body.

Notice and feel the appreciation you now have for your co-worker. Allow it into all the cells of your body. Let it permeate your whole being.

Feel free to write in your *Healing Notebook* about your experience of using the **Healing Process**—how you feel now, plus any actions you feel inspired to take.

My Healing Journey with a Co-Worker

I remember one time when I took a huge risk and stood up for myself not knowing if I would be fired on the spot.

I was a highly-trained Medical Ultrasonographer working in the perinatology department at a local hospital. My patients were women with high-risk pregnancies. Dr. Pierce, the head of the department, was extremely competent and respected, although I thought his bedside manner could use some work.

One afternoon shortly before lunch, I was doing an ultrasound on a new patient. Dr. Pierce entered the room, stood there observing the procedure, began criticizing my technique—in front of the patient—then turned and walked out.

As far as I knew, he had never done anything like that before to me, or anyone else—especially in front of a patient! In a New York minute, not only did I feel infuriated, embarrassed, and humiliated, I was appalled that the patient might think I was incompetent—I almost lost it!

After the patient left, I stormed down the hall and burst into Dr. Pierce's office to confront him about what just happened.

With every ounce of righteous indignation, I really let him have it.

"Don't you EVER reprimand me in front of a patient again. If I would have done that to you, you would have fired me on the spot. I consider you fired!"

"Oh, Victoria, you're way too sensitive."

"That's insulting! I'm NOT too sensitive. The only difference between you and me is you have a penis and more education—THAT'S IT! For your information, I am a qualified, certified, and highly-respected ultrasound technologist. You have no right to humiliate me like that. It's demeaning and I won't tolerate it. Anytime you feel the need to critique my work, feel free to set up a personal, private, training opportunity. I am not mistake proof and I'm willing to listen and learn."

"I see your point. I am sorry I spoke harshly to you in front of a patient. It was inappropriate," he admitted.

"OK, then, I accept your apology. In the future, please be more considerate. You may find that you'll get more of what you want or need from everyone who works with you through kind and thoughtful interactions."

"I get it, I'll give it my best," he said.

"Thank you. I need to go now. I have a lunch appointment."

"And, I have a patient waiting."

After this incident, our relationship became mutually respectful—I felt more like a colleague than a subordinate. Interestingly, when my birthday came around the next month, he gave me a $100 gift certificate. I believe that it was because I spoke up for myself and he had more respect for me.

The process of healing any relationship can be done energetically as described throughout the book, or it can happen spontaneously in person, as it did between Dr. Pierce and myself, or you could intentionally speak directly to anyone—your lips to their ears (not in a text or email)—to restore any relationship that is beneficial to you.

Final Thoughts

Healing your relationships in the workplace can provide a more harmonious environment with less conflict, stress, and anxiety, as well as greater job satisfaction with increased productivity.

For those who chose a co-worker who is still working with you, it could be interesting to see what naturally happens in your relationship. Now that you've begun the process of healing relationships with your co-workers—and the past is in the past where it belongs—don't be surprised if they reach out to you. Should there be anything left for you to say when they contact you, go ahead and communicate from your heart. No matter how the conversation ends up, it'll be more complete than before you began the **Healing Process.**

Remember to do something special for yourself as acknowledgment for the courage it took to heal the past with your co-workers. The difference you make in the lives of others is ultimately the difference you'll make in the creation of your magical life.

Supporting Your Child(ren) to Heal Their Relationships & Design Their Future

"Children are not a distraction from more important work. They are the most important work."

~ C.S. Lewis

After you've done most of your own healing work, it's time to work with the children in your life. Completing your own healing first, will help you to listen more intently to their heart-felt communication.

Are you a parent, step-parent, grandparent, foster parent, adoptive parent, godparent, aunt, or uncle? If so, keep reading.

Each child has a unique relationship with each person in their life and have their own dreams and desires no matter their age. You will be supporting them in releasing the harm they've received and designing what they want for their lives. Get together with each child individually. The **Healing Process** is basically the same as the one you've been using.

What an opportunity you will have to help your child(ren) heal their relationships with all of the people in their lives: you, other family members, people at school, people in the community, and people in their workplace (if they have jobs).

Read Chapter 3 with your child. Explain it in an age-appropriate way and ensure they understand what you'll be doing together. It's important to have your child release the harm caused by others in order to be successful in life.

I recommend sharing—with each child—the difference the **Healing Process** has made in your life, and hopefully it will motivate them to participate. Whatever works for each child is the way to proceed. They may want to do this totally on their own, or they may need you to do it with them, or they may decide not to do it at all. It's their choice. If they choose to participate, help them create a *Healing Notebook* before they begin, with a separate page for each person they want to include.

Helping Your Child(ren) Heal Their Relationships

Thirty-five years ago, when I was teaching parents how to massage their newborn babies, I learned about the three main elements of bonding: eye contact, focused attention, and touch. I encourage you to include all three while you are doing this process with your children, in order to experience a greater degree of love between you. As you proceed, let them know there is nothing wrong and they are safe to tell you whatever is on their mind or in their heart.

The process requires the ability to use one's imagination, and visualize or picture an object or action—which may be difficult for your child. To help your child visualize a person, place a photograph of the person in front of your child. To help your child imagine saying to a person, or imagine hearing a person saying to them—feel free to pretend you are that person.

Set aside enough time. Find a quiet, safe place where you won't be disturbed. Center yourself in the present moment. Tell your child to close their eyes, as you do the same. Tell your child to relax, get comfortable, and take a few deep breaths through their nose, as you do the same.

Have your child get out their *Healing Notebook*. Have them choose the relationship they want to heal. The relationship will determine which of the three following options to use. I suggest that you encourage them to begin with you.

Ask your child to choose an incident and tell you what happened. Capture their story in their notebook as they're recalling the experience. With the least amount of interruption and distractions, prompt for details (if necessary).

Healing Harm Others Caused Your Child

When Your Child Chooses to Heal with You

Let them know that nothing is too small—it could be something small in your world that looms large in theirs.

ASK *"Is there something I SAID that you'd like me to apologize for?"*

"Is there something I DID to you that you'd like me to apologize for?"

"Is there something I DIDN'T SAY—that would have made a difference for you—that you'd like me to apologize for?"

"Is there something I DIDN'T DO—that would have made a difference for you—that you'd like me to apologize for?"

"How did what happened make you feel?"

LISTEN and repeat what they told you. Take it in. Don't defend it at this time. They may not be sharing the truth about what happened, but it's their version and their experience of what occurred.

RECORD what happened in their notebook.

When Your Child Chooses to Heal with Another Child

Let them know that it's OK to talk about being threatened, bullied, teased, excluded, hit, etc. by other kids because it's safe here and now.

ASK *"Who has hurt you and never said, 'I am sorry?'"*

"How do you know this kid?"

"Where do they live?"

"What happened?"

"When did it happen?"

"Where did it happen?"

"How did what happened make you feel?"

LISTEN and repeat what they told you. Without emotion, don't judge or try to fix it at this time. They may not be sharing the truth about what happened, but it's their version and their experience of what occurred.

RECORD what happened in their notebook.

When Your Child Chooses to Heal with an Adult
Let them know that it's OK to talk about being threatened, scolded, inappropriately touched, etc. by an adult because it's safe here and now.
ASK *"Who has hurt you and never said, 'I am sorry?'"*
"How do you know this adult?"
"Where do they live?"
"What happened?"
"When did it happen?"
"Where did it happen?"
"How did what happened make you feel?"
LISTEN and repeat what they told you. Without emotion, don't judge or try to fix it at this time. They may not be sharing the truth about what happened, but it's their version and their experience of what occurred.
RECORD what happened in their notebook.

Support Your Child in Releasing Their Feelings
Let them know that it's safe to express their feelings in any way that works for them. The only rule is that they cannot harm themselves or others. Without interjecting your emotions, be open to the emotions that surface for them. As each feeling comes up, encourage them to REALLY express and release it by doing something like, crying into a pillow, hugging a pillow, punching a pillow, or screaming into a pillow.

Support Your Child in Freeing Themselves from the Harm You Caused Them
It's time now for your child to free him/herself from the harm associated with the experience. Have them repeat after you the following statement—to you:
> *"I'm no longer willing to keep the harm you caused me. I'm giving it back so you can make it up to me. I know you want to be the best you can be for me. Please, grant me your love and devotion so I can be free to create what I want in my magical life."*

Say to your child—with honor and respect:

> "I take back the shame, blame, and guilt. It's no longer necessary for you to suffer from the harm I caused you. I give you my love and devotion as a way to support you in moving forward in your life."

Support Your Child in Freeing Themselves from the Harm Another Child Caused Them, or the Harm an Adult Caused Them

It's time now for your child to energetically free him/herself from the harm associated with the experience. To help your child visualize the person use a photograph or tell them to close their eyes and visualize _____ (name of child/adult) standing in front of them. Have them repeat after you the following statement:

> "I'm no longer willing to keep the harm you caused me. I'm giving it back so you can make it up to me. I know you want to be best you can be. Please, grant me your best wishes so I can be free to create what I want in my magical life."

Tell your child that you are now pretending to be _____ (name of child/adult), and he/she is saying:

> "I heard what you said and I take back the shame, blame, and guilt. It's no longer necessary for you to suffer from the harm I caused you. I give you my best wishes as a way to support you in moving forward in your life."

Your Child Receives an Authentic Apology from the You (the Parent)

FIRST: Genuinely say to your child, *"I am sorry for _____ (what I said or didn't say; did or didn't do)."*

THEN: Tell your child what positive actions you will take to ensure the harmful behavior won't occur again.

FINALLY: Ask your child, *"How can I make it up to you and restore our relationship?"* Whatever your child asks you to do (within reason), agree to do it in a timely manner.

Your Child Receives an Authentic Apology from the Child/Adult
> FIRST: Tell your child to imagine _____ (name of child/adult) genuinely saying, "*I am sorry for* _____ *(what I said or didn't say; did or didn't do).*"
>
> THEN: Tell your child to imagine _____ (name of child/adult) saying what positive actions he/she will take to ensure the harmful behavior won't occur again.
>
> FINALLY: Tell your child to imagine _____ (name of child/adult) asking, "*How can I make it up to you and restore our relationship?*" Tell your child to picture what he/she needs and visualize _____ (name of child/adult) doing it.

Embrace the Healing

Make sure your child takes some time after healing each incident to integrate the experience. Ask them to breathe deeply through their nose to help them relax—suggest they breathe in love and breathe out any tension they may be holding in their body. Have them notice and feel the love or respect they now have for the other person.

Encourage them to write or draw in their *Healing Notebook* about their experience, how they feel now, or any actions they see they might take.

Support Your Child(ren) in Designing Their Future

As you are spending quality time with each of your children, I recommend that you encourage them to talk to you about what they want for their life. This supports them in articulating and sharing their dreams in a safe space and supports you in getting to know them at a deeper level. They will begin to understand how much you really care about their wishes, know that you are truly interested, and appreciate the attention they are receiving.

Children are mercurial and change their minds a lot, many times in the same day. So, go with the flow when your child—whose been dreaming and planning to be a ballerina for months—suddenly decides they want to be a race-car driver.

When you have family meetings or eat dinner together, one of the things you can discuss is what they've told you about what they want. You might ask, *"Is there anything special you want to do about your idea?" "Is there anything the family can help you with?"* This conversation also presents an opportunity for parents to talk about individual and family plans, such as vacations. Imagine how exciting your dinners or family meetings would be if this were the focus rather than what's not working and whose fault it is.

In the next chapter, we'll look at methods that help in creating great support structures for dreaming, goal setting, and designing their future.

A Child's Healing Journey

A friend shared this story about her childhood with me, and gave me permission to share it with you.

> *When I was in 1st grade, in Chicago, my school had an after-school program called, "Learn to Play the Piano." I really wanted to take lessons, so I asked my dad who said, "Before you can take lessons, you have to get straight 'A's on your report card." The years passed and finally in 7th grade I did it. My dad honored his word and let me take piano lessons. I was thrilled beyond belief!*
>
> *The classes and practice times were available at the school, so we didn't need to buy a piano. Dad just had to pay a fee. At the school music recital, my father recorded my performance and was shocked at how good I was. I still have that tape recording.*
>
> *At the end of the year, my teacher told me and my parents that I had real talent and was a quick study. She also told us, that she thought music and piano were something I should pursue.*
>
> *The next year we moved to another school where this program was not available. I was very disappointed until I noticed that our new next door neighbor had a grand piano and someone told me she gave lessons. One day after school, I knocked on her door and asked, "If I take lessons from you, can I practice on*

your piano?" She said, "Yes." I was so excited! I went home and told my dad. He became infuriated and yelled, "How dare you let the neighbors know that we can't afford a piano." He then made me lie to our neighbor by telling her that I couldn't take lessons because my schoolwork was more important, thus ending my piano career. The shame I experienced after that upsetting incident was unbearable.

Around this time, my 20-year-old sister, living in California, bought a piano and started taking lessons. Four years later the company she worked for transferred her to France. Before she left the country, she planned a short leave to come home for a month.

One night at dinner, about a week before my sister was due to arrive, my father announced, "I think we should buy a piano so Anna has a way to practice while she's here." He looked over at me and asked, "You play the piano too, don't you?" I was dumbfounded. I could only manage to nod my head as feelings of animosity, resentfulness, and outrage overwhelmed me. How could he not remember my impressive recital, the recording he made, and my teacher's acknowledgment? I just sat there and said nothing.

The very next day my parents and I went shopping for a piano. We ended up buying the most beautiful, shiny black, upright Baldwin—known by the slogan, America's Favorite Piano. I could not have been more delighted. While my sister may only be home for a month, that piano was going to remain in my living room—which meant I could play it anytime I wanted—and refuse to play it anytime my father was home.

After a couple of months, my mother noticed that whenever my father was in the house, I wouldn't play the piano at all, and if I was in the middle of practicing I would simply stop. What no one knew was that it was the only way I could punish my father for doing what he'd done to me—humiliating me and making me lie.

While my father was away on a weekend hunting tip, my

mother—the astute woman that she was—decided to broach the subject of my odd behavior. She sensed that I might be more open to explaining myself when he wasn't there. In her loving and understanding way, I eventually poured out everything I had held inside since I was five—the years I struggled to get straight 'A's. The shame I felt for lying to our neighbor. I yelled. I screamed. I pounded the table. I paced the floor. For over 20 minutes, I was sobbing so hard I could barely breathe. I even started to tear up my sheet music, but my mother stopped me.

When I had finally released all of my righteous indignation and I could talk normally again, she calmly said, "Your father has many peculiar rules. I'll have a talk with him." I asked her, "Do you think it's because he doesn't love me as much as he loves Anna? I don't remember what she said, because whatever she said, it wasn't my father saying it.

A few days later, the three of us talked about what happened and how I felt. I asked my dad why he did and said those things. He apologized and explained that he had made up the rules to avoid admitting he should have bought me a piano years ago.

I knew he deeply regretted his actions, he told me he loved me dearly, and as we hugged each other, I forgave him. I realize now that the opportunities I have had over the course of my life have been so much more rewarding than had I pursued a career in music. In spite of my dad's rules, I have made a real difference in the world.

Final Thoughts

Doing this healing work provides your child(ren) with the opportunity—now and throughout their lives—to be fully self-expressed, playful, happy, loving, spontaneous, confident, and free to be themselves.

Remember to do something special with your child(ren) as acknowledgment for the courage it took for them to heal with you and the people in their life.

11

Living a Magical Life

*"Imagination is more important than knowledge.
For while knowledge defines all we currently know and understand,
imagination points to all we might yet discover and create."*
~Albert Einstein

One of the reasons I wrote this book was to support forward-thinking individuals—and ultimately all of humanity—to free themselves from their suffering, struggling, bitterness, deep regret, and that which binds them to the past, so that they can live magical lives. It starts one person at a time. It starts with YOU. Acknowledge yourself for completing each process in each chapter so thoroughly. You are not the same person who began this book.

Today is the first day of the rest of your life. Now that you have most of your past in the past where it belongs, you can create something NEW. What are you yearning for? What does it look like to live an extraordinary, remarkable, and exceptional life? Or, perhaps you prefer an outstanding, incredible, phenomenal, and unbelievable life? Or, possibly a marvelous, astounding, amazing, astonishing, and fantastic life? Or, maybe you want a magnificent, wonderful, sensational, miraculous, fabulous, stupendous life? Or, instead, a life that is out of this world, terrific, awesome, and wondrous? Or, if you're like me, you dream about having a magical life!

If so, it's now time for you to design and manifest your magical life. I suggest dedicating a section of your *Healing Notebook* for this purpose.

Designing Your Magical Life

The three methods outlined in this section—visualizing, recording, and vision boarding—are all powerful ways to support you in designing your fabulous future.

You may choose to use all three, a combination, or just one. Explore—try one method then another—until you discover what works best for you. What's most important is to START!

Find a quiet, secluded place where you won't be disturbed. This is all about quieting the noise in your head so you can hear your heart reveal what you want for your life. Set aside as much time as you think you'll need to really focus on designing your magical life.

> *"The future is not someplace we are going, but one we are creating. The paths are not to be found, but made. And the activity of making them changes both the maker and the destination."*
> *~ John H. Schaar*

Start by setting the mood. Choose from the ideas below:
- Your sense of smell is very powerful. Consider using your favorite scented candle, an essential oil diffuser, or some incense.
- The sound of music by a performer that really lights up your soul can be inspiring. Consider choosing instrumental music so you won't be distracted or influenced by the lyrics.
- Peaceful meditation provides clarity. Consider connecting to your higher self, or call upon God for Divine guidance.

Close your eyes, take some slow deep breaths in and out through your nose, bring your energy and awareness down into your precious heart, and let the Source of All Creation support you.

Your magical life begins with intention. When you resonate with your intention, you become receptive to limitless possibilities—meeting the perfect people at the perfect time with the perfect opportunity. Consider including personal values, career, family, love life, health and well-being, entertainment, education, and personal growth. When your desires align with the energetic vibration of your magical life, you attract—or are attracted to—your intention.

Visualizing

Visualizing is a powerful way to generate what you want in your life. Even though it's only in your mind, the Source of All Creation recognizes what you desire and begins to provide what you need—when you need it.

Each person's experience of visualizing is unique. Many people see themselves participating in the images they create in their mind. Others see the pictures in front of them as if they are watching a movie on a white screen. Some hear sounds associated with the pictures, while others see symbols that represent their desires. There is no right or wrong way to visualize.

Start by saying, *"I am ready to see my heart's desires."* Then, allow the images of your future to come to you. Stop yourself from letting any limitations regarding money, time, energy, location, relationship status, current job/business, and family members, get in the way. Consider that whatever shows up is what your heart desires—you may be surprised by what emerges.

> *"Dare to visualize a world in which your most treasured dreams have become true."*
> ~ Ralph Marston

Visualize as many details as you can, like: Where are you? Who is with you? How old are you? How do you feel? What activities are happening?

Imagine you long to have a house on the beach. See it exactly as you want it to be: How many rooms? How is it decorated? What is the view? Can you see yourself moving through it? Can you smell the ocean? Can you feel the breeze? What kind of vehicle did you park in the driveway? What color is it? Keep going until everything you desire is in your mind's eye.

Recording

Get out your *Healing Notebook*. Capture the visualization that's in your mind's eye. Using the example above, consider starting by drawing a floor plan. Scribbling is good. Draw arrows to designate elements. Label significant features. Start writing a description of the house. Include all the meticulous details, finishes, and characteristics like: square footage, kitchen cabinets, knobs and pulls, appliances, countertops, flooring, furniture, spa-like bathrooms, mosaic tile, window coverings, a lanai, and deck chairs. Remember to describe the flavor, the mood, the textures, the romantic ambiance, as well as aspects of relaxation and entertainment. Details, details, details.

For those who are more comfortable using electronic devices to capture your visualization, start writing—it doesn't have to be chronological, it doesn't have to fit together, or even make sense—it's not a novel. Again, include as much and as many details as you can.

> "Writing is the painting of the voice."
> ~ Voltaire

When everything has been recorded, read through your intention and organize it—chronologically, or by subject: people, home, travel—or just leave it the way you wrote it.

Keep everything you've captured and recorded in one convenient place. Review it frequently and add to it as needed—whatever works best for you.

Vision Boards

A vision board is a display of your deepest desires, and when viewed every day, keeps you focused on your future—which is the key to manifesting your magical life.

Creating a vision board is more than simply cutting out magazine pictures and hoping for the best. It's a creative process based on INTENTION.

A vision board can be an actual poster or banner that is displayed on a wall, or a virtual image displayed on an electronic device. Choose the type of display that suits your lifestyle. Regardless of your preference, both need to contain—everything, everything, everything—every detail you recorded that you want in your magical life.

Start by classifying the main focus of your intention, e.g. freedom, vitality, abundance, balance, happiness, clarity, and gratitude.

The next step is to gather a collection of images, words, phrases, and affirmations that capture the essence of your vision. When you're satisfied that you have everything you need, let your intuition be a guide as you begin arranging your vision items—home, vehicle, money, career, relationship(s)—according to their relative importance (sized appropriately, if possible.)

This is your magical life. This is what you say you want. Go for it! Be creative! Get into it! Take your time. Enjoy the experience.

When it's complete, display it where you can see it every day. To increase the possibility of having what you desire, look at every detail of it for about 10 minutes. Reflect on why you chose those specific images and revisit the feelings of happiness and gratitude you felt when you created it. Viewing it often with your intention and attention on it, will forward the momentum toward achieving your magical life. Show it to those who matter most to you in life. Tell them what you're up to and request their support. For sharing and viewing purposes, save a copy on your phone.

"A vision is not just a picture of what could be; it is an appeal to our better selves to become something more."
~ Rosabeth Moss Kanter

This is after all, the 21st century, and there are other fun and interesting ways to create a unique, online vision boards using an electronic slideshow format—with music and voice-over capabilities! The sky's the limit!

Designing My Magical Life

It took about an hour to complete the first part of this process for designing my magical life, and this is what I did:

> *I went to my meditation/healing room in my home, where I knew I could have quiet time by myself. I began by getting comfortable in my chair, then took some slow deep breaths in and out through my nose. I brought my energy and awareness down into my precious heart and said to myself, "I am open and ready to see, feel, sense, and hear the magical future that is mine*

to have in alignment with divine guidance and my purpose." I let the thoughts and images flow.

I saw my perfect home; in the perfect location; with the right man who loves, cherishes, and adores me. My healing/coaching business is thriving, and I have the perfect referral partners. I have published six Amazon #1 best selling books. I sing weekly in the Higher Vibration Healing Choir, and my husband and I dance at the local studios, as well as travel together for pleasure and business, whenever and wherever we want—all of which feeds my soul.

> "Life holds special magic for those who dare to dream."
> ~ Author Unknown

My friendships are rich and meaningful. We have open and honest communication, we speak our truth, we hear and accept each other exactly as we are. We have fun together and support each other in accomplishing our dreams and goals—we even set each other straight, occasionally.

My body is strong, flexible, and fit, and I am vibrantly healthy Most importantly, I have deepened my relationship with God, and I receive daily guidance which I follow.

When I completed visualizing, I got out my Healing Notebook and wrote down everything I had seen in my mind's eye and I added a few more things that came in as I was writing. I knew that I was onto something when I was moved to tears as I let the words flow onto the paper.

The next step in this process, creating a vision board, took a bit more time. I gathered all the old magazines I had at home and shopped for a few more. I found and cut out a picture of a beautiful, plantation-style home that was located on a tropical peninsula overlooking a white, sandy beach. It felt like home.

I cut out pictures that revealed the many facets of the man of my dreams. In one picture, he was well-dressed sipping wine on the balcony of a Royal Caribbean cruise liner. Another picture showed him dancing, laughing, living and loving life at Mardi Gras. Yet another picture showed him in a tuxedo, standing at the altar with his best man, smiling from ear to ear. Woohoo!

Next, I found pictures of a woman speaking to an expansive audience. I was thrilled to find another picture showing a woman at a writing desk with a bookshelf displaying best-selling books behind her, and a picture of a woman being interviewed on a national morning TV show regarding her book tour.

I sprinkled the words: fun, romance, love, adventure, passion, and joy, around the pictures along with the phrases, "I declare it will happen," and "I proclaim it is mine." Every morning when I wake up, and every night as I am falling asleep, I feel blissful as I gaze at each picture I chose that embodies my magical life.

Manifesting Your Magical Life

You may have encountered people who just seem to get what they ask for without much apparent effort—things just drop into their lap—you might even have had this happen to you. This is the power of designing your life and manifesting your visualization using the universal law of attraction. This means that as soon you declare what it is you want, you will begin to see opportunities appear. Your job is to accept them with gratitude.

> "Whatever the mind can conceive and believe, the mind can achieve."
> ~ Napoleon Hill

Manifestation isn't magic, it takes some work. One way to improve your ability to have what you want is to create a project, or a series of projects, from the magical life you designed.

All manifestation begins with the end in mind. Get out your *Healing*

Notebook. Start designing a project with a specific outcome in mind from one area of your magical life. First, chose the date by which you will complete the project. Next, working backward through time, set at least three milestones to monitor your progress, each with a specified date. Declare each action step you need to take—from the end goal to each milestone. Determine the resources required for each step, e.g. materials, equipment, manpower, permits, etc. When all the steps have been identified, start the project.

Manifestation is not about expecting projects or desires to fall out of the sky. As you improve your ability to manifest, you may notice how much more smoothly project progress. Things may become more efficient and effective, with less stress, struggle and resistance. The time it takes to achieve the things you desire will appear swift and effortless—and that, my friends, looks like "falling into your lap."

Manifesting My Magical Life

Designing one aspect of my magical life was so much easier than the years of blood, sweat and tears it took to manifest it, and here's my story:

I wanted to make a difference in the lives of people through writing successful books. I'd never authored a book—how should I go about doing it? I was open to learning whatever it took.

Before starting any research, I visualized the project. I saw myself writing my books and being supported by a team of professionals. I visualized being a successful and well-respected author and saw people changing their lives through reading and practicing what I had written. I knew that being an Amazon #1 best-selling author was key to attaining credibility in this arena, so I visualized that too. Next, I wrote down, in great detail,

> "The secret to getting the breaks in life lies in knowing what, above all else, you want and in knowing how to weave the tapestry of your life so you get it."
> ~ Paul Keenan

everything I had visualized; then I created a fantastic vision board and put it on my desk so I could see my future every day.

The next logical thing to do was take action. I knew my friend, Dr. Margaret Mears, conducted a creative writing course, Write from Your Heart™, so I signed up. After completing that course, a book title, What Would Love Do Right Now?, popped into my mind—loud and clear. I grabbed a notebook. I wrote the title and my name on the first page and drew a big heart right in the middle. Easy peasy—I had a book cover! Hurray!

> "The day I decided that my life was Magical, there was suddenly Magic all around me."
> ~ Marabeth Quin Art

However, I couldn't seem to write anything for months and months. Back to the drawing board—or more succinctly, back to the vision board. I never stopped believing that my desire to write a book would happen.

Truth was I was overwhelmed by the idea of authoring a whole book—creative writing is one thing, completing a book is another. Out of the blue, a colleague suggested I attend Tom Bird's retreat, Write Your Book in 5 Days™. That sounded like just what I need—I thanked her, and God, for showing me the way. Back on track!

I researched the retreat and found that it was only 90 minutes away and within my budget, so I signed up. The day it started, I grabbed my original notebook and headed for Sedona. The workshop was intense, fun, and revealing. I completed the first draft of my first book during those five days—WOW! What a ride. Things are finally looking up.

But, now what? I had a rough draft, however, it was nowhere near being finished and my goal was to get my book onto the Amazon #1 Best-Seller list. YIKES! I knew nothing about how to do that. Then I found out that Tom Bird also offered a Publish Now Program which I thought had everything I needed to accomplish my goal. Nothing's going to stop me now! I was on my way and so excited to get started.

This is when my book finally became a bona fide project. I went home and created my production schedule. I chose the date I wanted to have my book available on Amazon. I wrote down all the things I needed to accomplish one month before the end date. I kept identifying what needed to be done month by month working backward until I reached the starting date of the Publish Now Program.

> "Vision without action is merely a dream. Vision with action can change the world."
> ~Joel A Barker

What surprised me the most was how manageable this project seemed to be. With everything written out on a timeline on a big poster board, I could envision its success—and most importantly—discovered I didn't have to accomplish everything the first month. It was apparent who I needed to call and when, as well as, who I needed to secure contracts with for different services that weren't included in Tom Bird's publishing package. I could now breathe in—as well as out!

Just when I thought it was safe to go back in the water, my ignorance bit me in the wallet. Being a new author, I hadn't known all the right questions to ask and I didn't know the difference between the terms, "copy editing" and "line editing." The Publish Now Program contract included copy editing only.

I was assigned a copy editor who I thought would be the answer to my prayers. After several months of working with him, going back and forth with little progress and lots of frustration, he informed me that what my book desperately needed was called "line editing" and it was going to cost me extra—A LOT extra.

The answer to my prayers was turning into a dispirited ordeal. The editor became less and less responsive and I realized he was not going to be able to finish the project. My expectations were thwarted. I felt so defeated I just gave up and stopped. Stick a fork in me—I'm done.

Every day I looked at my vision board—sitting there on my desk—reminding me of my sincere desire to make a difference in the lives of people by sharing the book I titled, What Would Love Do Right Now?

Knowing that the universal law of attraction is always working, I decided to focus on what I had declared, believe that it would happen, and expect opportunities to appear.

Soon after, God nudged me once more and I thought, "Let me try again." I contacted a colleague, who was also a writer, and she offered to edit my book with me. We spent four solid days together, during which time I had the feeling that she was taking "ME" out of my own book. She said things like, "This isn't true," "You can't say that," "I don't agree with your philosophy," "You need to update your approach," and then she added her own ideas. By now, I was so insecure about my ability as an author, I just broke down into tears and went home. Needless to say, I didn't use her version as my final manuscript. I was even more determined to forge ahead, aligned with my vision. Nothing could, or would, stop me now!

> "Where focus goes, energy flows."
> ~Tony Robbins

Fortunately, yet unbeknownst to me, two of my dearest friends while having lunch, were discussing the editing dilemma

I was having with my book—frankly, both of them were sick and tired of listening to all the problems I was having with editors—so they stepped up to the plate and offered to help me get my book out.

Betsy, who is a creative writer and award-winning graphic designer, polished my content and designed my book cover as well as my publishing website. Paula, who is an excellent editor, did everything from style editing to grammar, punctuation, and proofreading. Both are extraordinary wordsmiths.

With my dream team on-board, I established a new production schedule and we rolled up our sleeves and started right away. The three of us worked together diligently, burning the midnight oil, and turned my original rough draft into a fabulous manuscript ready to publish. We had a blast. It was magical!

We managed to format both the print and eBook versions on time. My print version went up first and got to #12, just through word of mouth by my family, friends, colleagues, and clients. I set about to find out what else I needed to do to get my book to #1.

Enter Denise Cassino. She works with authors and guarantees that their books achieve an Amazon #1 best-selling status. Sure enough, less than 24 hours after the eBook was available, it went to #1 and I became a best-selling author!!!

This credential gave me avenues to manifest my desire to make a difference in the lives of other people. I now have regular opportunities to speak to spiritual development groups, hold book-signings, and deliver workshops. I also facilitated a 10-week group forum, discussing and applying the principles from each chapter of my book. It made a significant difference in the lives of the participants, exactly what I wanted!

> "Find that magical place in your world...and live there."
> ~ Laura Loukaides

Final Thoughts

The people closest to you want you to have what you most want in life. Share with them your experience with the **Healing Process**, what you learned when designing your magical life, and show them your vision board. Tell them about how it's impacting you in the different areas of your life.

Doing this process with your whole family for a specific occasion or result is not only powerful, it can also be great fun. Vision boarding is also a wonderful way to make specific plans for projects, like taking a vacation, buying a new home, or running a marathon.

Doing this process with an intimate partner or someone special, is a good foundation for supporting each other's goals and dreams and creating a magical future together with grace and ease. You'll be amazed how much closer you feel. It will move your relationship to a whole new level of understanding, compassion, and love.

Conclusion

You can have a *Magical Life!* As you apply the concepts in this book and use the *Three Magical Words*, notice how your life becomes fuller and more magical in every way. Look everywhere for ways in which your life is improving.

Continue to set aside time to do this work on a regular basis, including with your children. In life things happen, and it's best to clean them up as soon as possible. This practice will support you in maintaining your well-being and sustaining loving and powerful relationships.

This book is based on cleaning up past relationships in my life. While I have only provided one example in each area of my life, I have used the process countless times. I have made many vision boards, some overarching, and some for only one specific future I wanted to manifest.

In the course of designing my magical life, so much more has opened up. Many things I visualized have come to fruition, and I have been granted opportunities I never imagined could or would be possible—those include:

I have deepened my relationship with God, and I receive daily guidance, which I follow. I have new friendships, which are deep, rich, and rewarding. I am singing up a storm, and dancing like nobody's watching! I have new referral sources for my business that recommend people who become my perfect, wonderful clients. I am taking action to ensure that my body is strong, flexible, and fit, and, as a result, I feel vibrantly ALIVE. I have declared that my perfect home will manifest—in the perfect location—as I am in action renovating several rooms in my house—which may determine whether I decide to love it or list it.

I have yet to manifest my fabulous husband, however I am in action, pursuing social interactions and introductions from friends.

Alfred A. Montapert once said, *"To accomplish great things, we must first dream, then visualize, then plan...believe...act!"* I urge you to follow the process and then ACT. Feel free to tell other people in your life about this process. Share with them the benefits you are experiencing, how much freer you feel, and all the ways your life is more magical. Encourage them to do the process for themselves so that they can create their own magical life.

Never, ever stop celebrating life with reckless abandon. Always and forever acknowledge the courage you possess to heal your past and restore each and every relationship in your life. Believe with all your heart that anything and everything IS possible!

It all starts with Three Magical Words and ends with A Magical Life!

Resources

Preface

    Benoit, Victoria M.C. *Owner, Center for Extraordinary Outcomes. Resonance Repatterning®*

        https://extraordinaryoutcomes.com/healing-methods/

What Are the Three Magical Words?

    Anderson, Uell Stanley. *Three Magic Words*

        https://www.amazon.com/Three-Magic-Words-Power-Plenty/dp/1773230662

Forgiveness and Making Amends

    Virtue, Doreen, PhD. *Healing With The Angels Oracle Cards, Forgiveness Card*

        https://www.amazon.com/Healing-Angels-Oracle-Cards-Large/dp/1561706396/

    Marmar, Stephen. *Forgiveness*

        http://www.prageru.com/courses/life-studies/forgiveness

    Hellinger, Bert. *Family Constellation According to Hellinger*

        https://www.hellinger.com/en/home/

The Healing Process

    Hay, Louise L. *You Can Heal Your Life*

        http://www.louisehay.com

Healing Your Relationships with People in Your Community

    Armstrong, Allison. *The Queen's Code®*

        http://www.understandmen.com

    Dispenza, Joe D.C. *Week Long Advanced Retreat*

        https://drjoedispenza.com/

Your Magical Life

Institute of Harmonic Science. *The Higher Vibrations, A Healing Choir*
https://highervibrationsmusic.com/

Benoit, Victoria. *"What Would Love Do Right Now? A Guide to Living an Extraordinary Life"*
https://extraordinaryoutcomespublishing.com/

Bird, Tom. *Write Your Book in a Weekend*
https://tombird.com

Cassino, Denise. *Best Seller Services*
http://www.bestsellerservices.com/

Acknowledgments

This book was made possible with the unwavering support of the following wonderful people who helped during the many phases of its birth. I begin by acknowledging myself for listening to my nudge to write and for my dedication and perseverance along the way. Next, Tom Bird, the book whisperer, and his wonderful staff who supported me. Finally, all my dear friends—especially, Rudrani Brand, Donna Maddox, LaRae Erickson, and Linda Green—all who have been at my side every step of the way.

With the deepest gratitude humanly possible, thank you to Paula Hofmeister, my extraordinary managing editor, a wordsmith whose unending attention to style and detail is off the charts; and to Betsy McGrew, my award-winning graphic designer, for her intuitive vision and relentless dedication to line editing, formatting, and designing my book cover, as well as my fabulous website, www.ExtraordinaryOutcomesPublishing.com.

I am who and where I am today due to the love of my mother, late father, and siblings—all silent supporters of my unique adventures, although often beyond their realm of conventional thinking—who support me just the same.

Last but not least, I extend profound appreciation to my biggest fan, my late beloved husband, Bernie, whose unconditional love for me and outstanding support for my greatness has been a solid foundation from which I continue to discover and explore—the writer within.

About the Author

I'm Victoria Benoit—Personal Development Coach using Resonance Repatterning as well as an Amazon #1 Bestselling Author and Publisher—residing in Phoenix, Arizona. I am a fun-loving, optimistic woman living an extraordinarily rich life, filled with passion, love, and adventure.

Along with writing, speaking, and facilitating transformational healing, I enjoy West Coast Swing, Ballroom, and Country dancing; singing; biking; hiking; spending time in nature; and traveling to beaches around the world.

My friends and family are especially dear to me no matter what we're doing together. My biggest fan for the ten years we were together, was my Beloved Bernie, who liberated his soul from his physical body on November 27, 2017.

I grew up in Milwaukee, WI, with my younger brother and two sisters. When I was 20 years old, I seized an opportunity to move to the big city of Chicago—knowing no one—relying solely on my own sense of adventure.

The next 16 years were both routine and eventful. While having a successful career in medical ultrasound and being married and divorced, I began my journey of personal growth and transformation.

In 1989, I decided it was time to move on—from the Windy City to the Valley of the Sun—Phoenix. Shortly after moving, I was forced to change careers due to a physical injury at work. In examining what to do next, I saw that through my work as a neonatal ultrasound technologist, I had experienced my natural ability to provide a space of profound love and compassion for couples in the initial stage of grief over the loss of their baby. I applied this insight to create a new career in supporting people through tough times.

The next step in my journey was to obtain my master's degree and begin working as a Licensed Professional Counselor. I was quickly frustrated with my clients' lack of progress using traditional methodologies. I decided to study other approaches to support people in creating lives they loved. This guided me to become a Certified Resonance Repatterning® practitioner and teacher. I then began working part time with private clients, helping them to identify and clear their unconscious patterns. Session after session they reported experiencing extraordinary outcomes in their lives.

Based on my results with private clients, I left traditional counseling completely in 1996, and opened the Center for Extraordinary Outcomes. Along with seeing clients, I started teaching Resonance Repatterning domestically and internationally; I developed workshops; and continued to study and implement additional holistic healing therapies in my practice.

Over the years, it became apparent that I needed to stop teaching and start writing to fulfill my desire to impact even more people.

I absolutely love the difference I make in the world! I am committed to helping people live their magical life—one that is overflowing with love, joy, passion, and fulfillment.

Stay Connected

Thank you for purchasing this book. I trust you enjoyed it. To inspire others, please write a review and share an extraordinary outcome that made a difference in your life on Amazon.com, Goodreads.com, and/or ExtraordinaryOutcomesPublishing.com.

Be the first to hear about my new releases and bargains. Sign up at the link provided below to be on the VIP list.

I promise not to share your email with anyone or clutter your inbox.
http://www.ExtraordinaryOutcomesPublishing.com/stay-connected/

For more information about my transformational healing work, visit my website at: https://www.extraordinaryoutcomes.com/

About Book One

Living from your heart is possible! Asking yourself, *"What would love do right now?"* can be as impactful to your life as Jack Canfield's Chicken Soup is to his readers' souls.

In this step-by-step guide to living an extraordinary life, Victoria shares her philosophy about the power of love, forgiveness, making amends, and emotional healing in those areas and relationships that effect your quality of life today—family, career, romance, health, finances, and self-expression. You will be able to release and heal the pain and suffering from past heartaches, disappointments, and failures that undermine your ability to manifest your dreams and prevent you from living the life you were born to live.

Extraordinary lives are filled with adventures that have a beginning, middle and end; however, asking the question, *"What would love do right now?"* is always useful at any time, in any place, and with anyone—forever.

https://extraordinaryoutcomespublishing.com/what-would-love-do-right-now/
https://www.amazon.com/What-Would-Love-Right-Extraordinary/dp/0983856702/

www.ingramcontent.com/pod-product-compliance
Lightning Source LLC
Chambersburg PA
CBHW072052290426
44110CB00014B/1657